P9-EMB-788

Gil G. Noam
Editor-in-Chief

NEW DIRECTIONS FOR YOUTH DEVELOPMENT

Theory
Practice
Research

fall | 2005

Community Schools

A Strategy for Integrating Youth Development and School Reform

Joy Dryfoos
Jane Quinn

issue
editors

JOSSEY-BASS ™
An Imprint of
WILEY

COMMUNITY SCHOOLS: A STRATEGY FOR INTEGRATING YOUTH DEVELOPMENT
AND SCHOOL REFORM
Joy Dryfoos, Jane Quinn (eds.)
New Directions for Youth Development, No. 107, Fall 2005
Gil G. Noam, Editor-in-Chief

Microfilm copies of issues and articles are available in 16mm and 35mm, as well as micro-
fiche in 105mm, through University Microfilms Inc., 300 North Zeeb Road, Ann Arbor,
Michigan 48106-1346.

NEW DIRECTIONS FOR YOUTH DEVELOPMENT (ISSN 1533-8916, electronic ISSN 1537-5781)
is part of The Jossey-Bass Psychology Series and is published quarterly by Wiley Subscription Services, Inc., A Wiley Company, at Jossey-Bass, 989 Market Street, San Francisco,
California 94103-1741. POSTMASTER: Send address changes to New Directions
for Youth Development, Jossey-Bass, 989 Market Street, San Francisco, California
94103-1741.

SUBSCRIPTIONS cost $80.00 for individuals and $180.00 for institutions, agencies, and
libraries. Prices subject to change. Refer to the order form at the back of this issue.

EDITORIAL CORRESPONDENCE should be sent to the Editor-in-Chief, Dr. Gil G. Noam,
Harvard Graduate School of Education, Larsen Hall 601, Appian Way, Cambridge, MA
02138 or McLean Hospital, 115 Mill Street, Belmont, MA 02478.

Cover photograph © Bill Foley.

www.josseybass.com

Contents

 1. Full-service community schools: A strategy—not a program   7
    Joy Dryfoos
    The concept that drives the emerging full-service community school
    movement is this: Schools cannot address all the problems and needs of dis-
    advantaged children, youth, and families. Community schools are operated
    jointly by school systems and community agencies, are open extended
    hours, and may provide the site for after-school programs, primary-care
    health services, mental health counseling, parent education and involve-
    ment, and community development. No two community schools are alike.
    They grow out of a planning process that involves all stakeholders, school
    personnel, community-based organizations, city and county government,
    parents, and students. The Quitman Street Community School in Newark,
    New Jersey, exemplifies this approach.

 2. The Children's Aid Society community schools: A full-service
    partnership model   *15*
    Jane Quinn
    In 1989, the Children's Aid Society (CAS) created an unprecedented part-
    nership with the New York City Board of Education by developing a com-
    prehensive response to the pressing needs of children and families in the
    northern Manhattan neighborhood of Washington Heights. After three
    years of careful planning, CAS and the New York City public schools
    opened the first community school at Intermediate School 218, offering a
    full array of supports, services, and learning opportunities. Adding, on
    average, one partnership school per year and remaining very flexible in
    adapting its model to the individual needs of each community, CAS now
    has thirteen community schools around New York City. The model's
    flexibility is seen also in the success of its national and international
    adaptation—an intentional part of CAS's work.

community schools. By engaging broad constituencies across communities, LEFs have been able to build strong relationships between and among community institutions under a common vision.

In partnership with Chicago's public and private sectors, Chicago Public Schools (CPS) has successfully implemented a citywide education reform effort, designed to transform Chicago's neighborhood schools into vibrant centers of the community. Mayor Richard M. Daley and Arne Duncan, CEO of CPS, launched the Community Schools Initiative in January 2002. What started as an idea that was developed by a local foundation has now grown into the largest-scale community school effort in the nation, with sixty-seven schools in operation and a plan to move to one hundred community schools by 2007. This initiative currently involves seventeen private funders, ten technical assistance providers, thirty-four community-based organizations that offer on-site services to children and families, and over three hundred additional community partnerships that provide one-day events such as health fairs and violence prevention workshops.

A model of community-school partnerships is developing within a school district in Evansville, Indiana. Based on a full-service community school philosophy, the model started in one elementary school in the Evansville-Vanderburgh School Corporation and has expanded into a districtwide initiative called the School Community Council. The council is made up of over seventy community organizations and social service agencies working together to establish full-service schools as places of community and to enhance youth and family development.

Leaders of full-service schools in Boston seek to expand the number and increase the impact of Boston's full-service schools, catalyzing a realignment of public resources and an expansion of private investment. The Full-Service Schools Roundtable, led by a dynamic staff and supported by the mayor and the superintendent of schools, is a steadily growing coalition of educators, public agencies, human service providers, and community leaders. Challenges for the Roundtable are to build the public will to invest in full-service schools; secure leadership from stakeholders; share accountability across sectors so that schools prioritize youth development and health, and service providers share responsibility for school success; and become a political force, championing the strategic realignment of public investments based on child outcomes.

Editor-in-Chief's Notes

New schools for a new era: Catching up to a new social, health, and educational reality

THIS VOLUME, edited by two of the most respected leaders of the community school and full-service school movements, Joy Dryfoos and Jane Quinn, represents a testimony to the progress of the past years. In city after city across the United States, educators, activists, foundation staff, donors, and civic leaders have introduced and supported pilot schools, model programs, and demonstration sites. To introduce individual schools is very important but typically does not represent a full-community approach. The work is now making a transition from pilots and demonstration phases to a systemic approach encompassing entire school districts, health services, universities, and youth-serving organizations. This is, indeed, good news and deserves a status report about the field, the different strategies for partnering, and how sustainability could be accomplished.

So what have the participants of this social and educational experiment been learning? This question is at the heart of our current issue of *New Directions for Youth Development.*

Full-service and community schools are both important because they address a large part of a young person's waking hours—the obligatory school time and the choice-based out-of-school time. This "double institutionalization" can make for greatly dysfunctional experiences for a young person, but it does not have to be that way; fortunately, prolonged time in a social institution can lead to many good outcomes.

The dangers inherent in full service long days in school are rarely mentioned in the literature and oblige practitioners and policymakers to build a new sense of engaged time for an all-day

NEW DIRECTIONS FOR YOUTH DEVELOPMENT, NO. 107, FALL 2005 © WILEY PERIODICALS, INC.

experience. This new day finally corresponds to the realities of working families who need safe and educationally rich settings for their children. This long day in a young person's life cannot just extend the school hours, as many politicians are calling for, but requires an innovative approach to making these environments rich and explorational, as well as choice- and voice-oriented.

The goal of extending the day without creating a longer traditional school day is embraced by a large movement of after-school education and care that uses this journal as a central outlet. After-school programs are not necessarily part of the community and full-service school movements, but they are often the first step in the creation of such schools. It is very important to develop a plan of collaboration and coordination between these two significant movements. Opinions about how to do this often differ considerably. After-school intermediaries in different cities and large organizations that serve youth after school often believe that it is difficult enough to establish good after-school programs without engaging all the other institutions and issues, such as mental health, health, social services, family programming, nutrition, legal services, and so on. They know of the importance of these issues but want to first get the after-school part "right."

Full-service and community school protagonists often agree with this tactical point of view but believe that the problems facing children, families, and teachers cannot be solved without active community involvement. They also believe that the school needs to become a center where the barriers to health and mental health services are reduced and where parents and siblings find a home away from home. Even the best after-school program cannot address all of these issues, but full-service schools potentially can.

Thus an important question arises: What are the risks and benefits to taking one of two roads: (1) to map out a full-service and community agenda but begin with an after-school program that has the seeds of the larger vision already implanted (for example, inclusiveness of all children, staff trained to detect mental health needs, strong parent involvement, and so on), or (2) develop an after-school program that serves the needs of young people as an after-school program and, as it matures, incorporate other aspects of a full-service school when capacity and funding become available? From this perspective a good after-school program is by itself a possible step toward a community and full-service school without incorporating any full-service components.

This issue has to be at the center of any strategic thinking about community schools. Although there remains a significant amount of apprehension by educators about the management issues of community schools, after-school as a new social space that is needed in every school and every community has become a widely accepted reality. Many principals are daunted by the organizational complexity of running full-service schools and sometimes are very worried about true community input into their school. But they typically recognize that parents work and that children are not safe on the streets or by themselves at home. They also recognize the need for help with homework. Even this kind of organizational extension poses a great deal of apprehension for school personnel, but it seems more manageable than all other matters of social, health, and adult development practices. It does not help that schools of education have by and large ignored the new social realities and are training teachers and principals as if we still live in an old order.

As this volume attests, the voices for a fuller approach to the needs of children and their families than after-school programs can supply are on the rise. The typical superintendent, principal, and teacher recognize that the educational mission of schools can only be reached if hunger, child abuse, deportation, homelessness, incarceration—all-too-typical experiences in urban and poor rural environments—are responded to "in the best interest of the child." But it is one thing to recognize modern realities of families and children and another thing to manage a setting that addresses some of these social ills and personal tragedies. Even if all the community organizations and the available services congregate in the school and make it a living hub of human concern and collective problem solving, the one who has to coordinate "the traffic" and fully buy in is the principal and her superior—the district superintendent. That is how the bureaucratic power lines are established and maintained.

The need to establish lines of power brings us to the issue of training leaders and teachers. There is, at present, no clear set of trainings in full-service schools for future superintendents, principals, teachers, and guidance counselors. It is an urgent matter to create such materials and training institutes and to do so across universities and colleges in the form of consortia that can have a wide and immediate impact. We need a new educational workforce that can manage this new educational entity. We also need to spend time on providing technical assistance to existing schools and leaders, as the Children's Aid Society (CAS) has done so productively over the past decade. But the needs are overwhelming, and no single institution can address them alone.

Full-service and community schools are essentially collaborative enterprises. It is high time for us, as practitioners in the field, as policy makers and researchers, to develop training and technical assistance, as well as good theory and research on the issue of partnership. Partnering is like being in a committed relationship or marriage—one of the essential tasks most adults want to solve productively and one that can create the difference between heaven and hell on earth—and yet one that no one gets trained for. Partnerships are maybe not as intense, but the success of any enterprise depends on a trusting, fair, and healthy collaboration. Check any university or college Web site, and you will see the paucity of courses on this topic. How much more successful we could be if we had some training and did not have to make each mistake all over again and could simply pass on the earnings from our victories!

And victories are many, as this volume of *New Directions for Youth Development* demonstrates. We can be proud that so many dedicated, creative, and intelligent people have banded together in municipality after municipality to make a reality out of a dream. If we could save only one child from despair and suicide, provide one family with help gaining legal status, or help one struggling reader become fluent, the effort would be worthwhile. But the impact of increasing the numbers of full-service community schools and new legislation will touch millions of children, youth, and families, and we will have created deep reform of separate systems that can achieve their goals only together.

Gil G. Noam
Editor-in-Chief

Issue Editors' Notes

THIS VOLUME should help spread the word about community schools. In it, major initiatives taking place across the country are described by the leaders of these efforts, who have agreed to serve as authors. Chapters Two, Three, Four, and Five describe four different approaches to community schools, starting with the comprehensive Children's Aid Society model, which has been widely replicated. Beacons attempt to transform schools by placing community-based youth development workers in the school building for extended hours. The university-assisted model uses both faculty and students to enrich the local schools and draws on the community as a laboratory. The Public Education Network builds on all these strategies to encourage their local education funds to facilitate the "marriage" between schools and community agencies.

Chapters Six through Nine document the process of adapting these models and going to scale. The Chicago school system has made a substantial commitment to the community school strategy, with a view toward opening one hundred sites within the next five years. In Portland, Oregon, city and county officials strongly back the Schools Uniting Neighborhoods initiative across six school districts. The Evansville, Indiana, effort started with one school and is now replicated across the district with a wide array of stakeholders. Boston recently organized the Full-Service Schools Roundtable, with a view toward helping all schools form partnerships and bring in needed services.

Chapters Ten and Eleven focus on policy issues. The experience implementing California's Healthy Start legislation over two

NEW DIRECTIONS FOR YOUTH DEVELOPMENT, NO. 107, FALL 2005 © WILEY PERIODICALS, INC.

decades provides insights into this process. Finally, the head of the Coalition for Community Schools offers his view of the policy, regulatory, and funding implications of a rapidly developing social movement.

Joy Dryfoos
Jane Quinn
Editors

JOY DRYFOOS *is an independent writer from Brookline, Massachusetts.*

JANE QUINN *is assistant executive director for community schools at the Children's Aid Society in New York City.*

Community schools are one solution to the fact that "schools can't do it alone." Today's youth need comprehensive, coordinated support services provided in schools through partnerships.

1

Full-service community schools: A strategy—not a program

Joy Dryfoos

WHAT ARE "full-service community schools," and what do they have to do with youth development? Community schools are those that have been intentionally transformed into neighborhood hubs and that are open all the time to children and their families. In these buildings, a range of support services is provided by community agencies to help overcome the many barriers that schools face in producing successful students. What makes these schools different is that they are operated through partnership agreements between public schools and community agencies. They are not to be confused with charter schools, which operate outside the formal school system. These are regular public schools that are undergoing transformation within the system.

Advocates for full-service community schools believe that today's schools cannot possibly take on all the problems of today's children and their parents. The pressures from No Child Left Behind are enormous, draining teachers' energy and demoralizing administrators, who recognize that there is more to education than testing. Schools need other agencies to share some of the responsibility.

NEW DIRECTIONS FOR YOUTH DEVELOPMENT, NO. 107, FALL 2005 © WILEY PERIODICALS, INC.

They need help being open all the time, including before and after school, evenings, weekends, and summers. They want access to comprehensive support services, including primary-care health clinics, dentistry, mental health counseling and treatment, family social work, parent education, enhanced learning opportunities, community development, and whatever else is needed in that school community. One of the mantras of this emerging field is "no two alike"; each community school evolves according to the particular needs and resources of the population and the neighborhood.

Benefits for youth development

We know that young people thrive when they are surrounded by supportive adults and effective parents. The most fundamental concept in healthy child development is attachment. A child must have access to a responsible adult, if not a parent, as well as someone like a teacher, mentor, or counselor. This concept is actualized by bringing into the school building both practitioners and parents to supplement the teaching and support staff already in place. The goal of full-service community schools is to generate a truly child-centered environment. Efforts can start with very young children and continue all the way through lifetime learning for parents and grandparents.

Early intervention

The importance of pre-K programs is now widely recognized, especially for disadvantaged children to begin the process of learning and living with other people. Children require attention from their earliest years, and this must be sustained as they go through school. Increasingly, practitioners are focusing on pre-K–12 clusters of community schools.

Access to ongoing supports, services, and opportunities

The positive youth development approach revolves around several key constructs: that young people have, and are developing, assets as they move toward productive adulthood; that young people are agents of their own development, not just passive recipients of services, and that all young people need ongoing access to positive developmental supports, services, and opportunities as they move through childhood and adolescence. By their very nature and definition, community schools are a perfect strategy for promoting positive youth development because they dramatically increase the developmental assets available on a regular basis to young people and their families.

Parent involvement

We have accumulated a lot of experience in how to involve parents in schools. The first point of contact can be outreach into the home, that is, inviting the family into the school community and helping parents understand the way the school works. Community schools can offer a wide array of programs and services, with particular attention to cultural differences and language barriers.

Community involvement

Because community schools encompass the whole neighborhood, these new institutions are interested in community development. In some of these schools, the surrounding area serves as a laboratory for studying the environment, history, and sociology, while in other schools, the students learn by giving service to community groups such as senior citizens or nursery schools.

An exemplary community school

One has only to visit a fully implemented community school to see the warm and stimulating environment that collaboration can produce. The Quitman Street Community School (preschool–4) in Newark, New Jersey, is an example of a community school with a strong lead agency—Community Agencies Corporation of New Jersey—and a comprehensive family involvement component.[1] The school building is teeming with activity; parents are involved in the classroom, on the playground, and in the cafeteria. After-school activities are designed to extend what goes on in the classroom.

Teachers, parents, and school and agency support workers confer with each other to ensure that every child can function well within the school system. Parents are encouraged to "hang out" in the parent resource room, where they have access to computers, food, and advisers, as well as support and friendship with each other. Family members have access to trained medical personnel, including dentists, in a well-equipped clinic; social workers are on the site. The students perform better under these circumstances and clearly feel better in the vastly improved school climate. The neighborhood has improved as well, with a new playground designed by the students and constructed by neighborhood residents and corporate volunteers, and a street clean-up campaign organized by the parents.

In successful community schools, the community agency personnel and the school-oriented parents bring a strong youth development perspective into the school environment. Although teachers and administrators know that they must address the developmental needs of children and youth, they welcome the additional "hands" to work with them on the hands-on approaches required. Personal attention takes time. So does coordination.

One key to the success of schools like Quitman is the presence of a full-time coordinator—in this case supplied by the lead agency, who acts as a peer to the principal. The coordinator takes on the job of organizing the support services and involving the parents. Together with the principal, the coordinator works to integrate these activities with what goes on in classrooms. The principal is freed up to concentrate on academic achievement, which is, after all, the central purpose of the school.

From concept to social movement

The concept of community schools is not really new; these ideas of collaboration and community orientation have been around for over a century. However, the current version is more complex than in the past, probably because the problems and pressures are greatly heightened and because young people need a higher level of development than ever before if they are to have the skills necessary in contemporary adulthood. No other generation has had to deal with the strong arm of the No Child Left Behind Act, which is forcing schools to concentrate on "teaching to the test" and making pariahs out of students, teachers, and schools labeled as "failing."

The current crop of community schools has grown out of adversity, with the decay of the inner city and the widening of the achievement gap. Around 1990, various models began to emerge from around the country in a surge of spontaneous innovation. Those working independently to bring support services and outside community agencies into schools and enrich the intellectual and social environment included social workers at the Children's Aid Society (CAS) in New York; faculty at the University of Pennsylvania in Philadelphia; city and county officials in Portland, Oregon; health providers and private foundations in California; state officials in Florida and New Jersey, and a school principal in Evansville, Indiana. The leaders of these efforts came together in 1998 under the auspices of the Institute for Educational Leadership, in Washington, D.C. The Coalition for Community Schools was launched and now has 170 participating organizations representing the educational establishment and unions, youth development organizations, health and welfare agencies, and other interested parties. Through the coalition platform, school and youth development people can communicate with and learn from each other.

Progress to date

The community school concept does not yet have wide recognition in the educational world. School reformers are just beginning to acknowledge its importance and to incorporate "collaboration" into their thinking. Envision a continuum of services from a single activity, such as an after-school program, to the whole package, such as the Quitman Street Community School. These single activities are avenues to the fully developed model, and they are rapidly proliferating.

After-school programs have received the most attention, at least from the federal government. More than seven thousand schools have received grants through the billion-dollar annual expenditures of the 21st Century Community Learning Centers program to open the schoolhouse doors in the afternoons and summers, frequently under the auspices of community-based youth agencies such as Boys & Girls Clubs, Y's, and other nonprofits. At least fifteen hundred schools have primary health care clinics, with services provided by local community health centers or hospitals. It has been estimated that more than five thousand family resource centers are located in schools. These are, of course, central pieces to the whole package but without further development will not significantly change the climate of the school. They will remain "add-ons" that are dropped into the building without integration with what goes on in the classroom and therefore will not significantly affect the outcomes.

The "further development" is the real challenge to both youth development workers and educators. At the moment, the constituent components of community schools are ensconced in their own domains or silos. For example, educators come out of schools of education with little knowledge of youth development and behavioral psychology. Social workers come out of schools of social work with virtually no exposure to what goes on in classrooms. Yet for contemporary youth to be served, each domain has to be entered and mastered by the other.

The "lead agency" is a vital partner in this enterprise and usually hires the on-site coordinator—the person responsible for putting all the pieces together and making sure that they are integrating into the school. The coordinator works closely with the principal to interpret the community school strategy and spirit to the school staff. The lead agency personnel and other outside staff brought in to perform various functions must also learn how to operate within the school's culture and procedures. It is particularly important for teachers to be oriented toward community schooling and learn to benefit from the services offered.

But the arrangements that will put all these pieces together take time. A needs-and-resource assessment must be conducted to determine what already exists and what is needed. An oversight committee must be formed, representing teachers, support personnel, administrators, parents, and even students, as well as the community. The plan that emerges can take more than a year of dialogue, starting with an educational process about the concepts and including specifications about who will do what and who will pay for whatever is done.

Going to scale

We are convinced that the concept underlying community schools is important to the healthy development of millions of young people. They cannot succeed in schools that are failing. Schools need help from community agencies, not only to provide support services but to change the environment and climate of the school building. Innovative initiatives are under way all over the country (and in many other countries as well), but going to scale represents a major challenge in most cities. An entire school system must embrace this strategy and be willing to let the "outsiders" in. City and county agencies have to be willing to share their resources and their personnel.

Prognosis for the future

Repeated attempts to introduce legislation at the federal level have not gotten very far. Everyone is so fixated on No Child Left Behind that it is difficult to find sponsorship for even a small appropriation for the development of community schools. Yet despite budget cuts and uncertainties, there are still categorical sources that can be tapped for different components of community schools.

I believe that the future of community schools lies in two places: (1) the strength of the demand that emanates from the local level and (2) the high quality of the people all around the country who are responding to that demand. It is encouraging to observe how quickly both school and community agency personnel respond to the full-service community school strategy when they are exposed to it. An educational process is under way to instruct the appropriate stakeholders that, if they develop collaborative relationships, they heighten the chances of achieving their mutual goals. School personnel and parents must get together and recognize that their communities can become more responsive to the developmental needs of the children.

Note

1. Quitman Street Community School. (2004). *Five year report*. Newark, NJ: Prudential Foundation.

JOY DRYFOOS *is an independent writer from Brookline, Massachusetts.*

Joint planning and committed leadership have led to a long-term partnership between several New York City public schools and the Children's Aid Society, with positive results for children, families, and neighborhoods.

2

The Children's Aid Society community schools: A full-service partnership model

Jane Quinn

IN 1989, the Children's Aid Society (CAS)—New York City's oldest and largest youth-serving organization—created an unprecedented partnership with the New York City Board of Education by developing a comprehensive response to the pressing needs of children and families in the northern Manhattan neighborhood of Washington Heights. After three years of careful planning, CAS and the New York City public schools opened the first community school at Intermediate School (I.S.) 218, offering a full array of supports, services, and learning opportunities that include after-school enrichment (academic, social, cultural, and recreational), parent involvement, adult education, child health insurance enrollment, medical and dental services, mental health services, immigration and other legal assistance, summer camp, community events, and economic development. Adding, on average, one partnership school per year, CAS now has thirteen community schools (five

NEW DIRECTIONS FOR YOUTH DEVELOPMENT, NO. 107, FALL 2005 © WILEY PERIODICALS, INC.

elementary schools, seven intermediate schools, and one high school) in four New York City neighborhoods—Washington Heights, East Harlem, South Bronx, and Staten Island.

The overarching goal of the CAS model of community schools is to promote children's learning and development in ways that prepare them for productive adulthood. Recognizing that children's learning and development are influenced by their ongoing experiences in their families, schools, and communities, CAS community schools work to integrate the efforts of all three of these major influences through a partnership approach that addresses five outcome areas: students, families, school, community, and education policy.

The CAS model has three distinguishing characteristics:

1. *Comprehensiveness:* Its full-service approach is designed to address the multiple needs of children and families.
2. *Coherence:* Joint planning and decision making involve the major partners (school, CAS, and parents) and intentionally seek to integrate all aspects of the community school, particularly the school-day academic program and the before- and after-school enrichment program.
3. *Commitment:* CAS and its partner schools make a long-term commitment to work together with and on behalf of students and their families.

Another hallmark of the CAS model is its flexibility. In New York City, the model has several variations. For example, two of the elementary schools (Public School [P.S.] 5 and P.S. 8) have Early Head Start and Head Start programs operated by CAS that facilitate a seamless transition for young children as they move from preschool to elementary school. Another benefit of this approach is that parents become comfortable in the school when their children are very young, and many continue their involvement throughout their children's elementary education.

The model's flexibility is seen also in national and international adaptation—an intentional part of CAS's work. Since 1994, CAS has operated a National Technical Assistance Center for Community Schools. Over seven thousand visitors have come to see and learn from our New York City schools since that time, resulting in the adaptation of the CAS model in over one thousand schools, nationally and internationally. Many of these adaptation sites have been pleased to learn that CAS developed its model on a very solid research base, including studies that address the following factors: child and adolescent development,[1] parent involvement,[2] out-of-school-time experiences and their particular importance for low-income children,[3] after-school programs for elementary-age children,[4] community-based development programs for teenagers,[5] consistent adult guidance and support,[6] community influences,[7] service coordination,[8] and, finally, community schools as an integrative approach.[9]

Core components: The practice

Working with its Department of Education (DOE) colleagues, CAS conceptualizes its approach as a "developmental triangle" that incorporates three interconnected support systems into one core structure: (1) a strong core instructional program designed to help all students meet high academic standards; (2) enrichment activities designed to expand students' learning opportunities and to support their cognitive, social, emotional, moral, and physical development, and (3) a full range of health and mental health services designed to safeguard children's well-being and remove barriers to learning. Although programs vary from school to school, all CAS community schools follow this broad framework and tailor the specifics of their program to the needs of the students and their families. A structured needs-and-resource assessment initiates each partnership and is updated periodically. Ongoing joint planning is conducted at each school through formal vehicles, including the School Leadership Team (a mandatory governance structure in the New York City public schools that involves school administrators and faculty, parents and, as appropriate, community partners like CAS).

Across the CAS schools, the following services are offered:

• *After-school programs:* Youth-oriented enrichment programs include arts, sports, and community service, as well as a variety of educational enrichment such as chess clubs, science clubs, and recycle-a-bicycle programs. Many of these enrichment programs use outside resources like KidzLit (a literacy enrichment program created by the Developmental Studies Center), Foundations (another literacy enrichment program), and Project Learn (from Boys & Girls Clubs of America). These programs are offered on a daily basis all year long.

• *Summer camps:* Ten of the thirteen schools offer summer camps. Unlike after-school programs, which typically operate three hours per day, these programs span an eight-to-ten-hour day, providing young people with more intensive and varied experiences such as opportunities to explore the outdoors and trips to cultural and recreational venues. Day camps typically have themes, such as the Teen Travel Camp at I.S. 218 and Oh, The Places You'll Go!—a literacy enrichment camp at P.S. 5 that focuses on Dr. Seuss. CAS also offers specialty camps, such as the Alvin Ailey Dance Camp at I.S. 90, which draws campers from across the city. In recent years, all CAS community school camps have found ways to combine academics with social, cultural, and recreational enrichment, in view of the fact that "summer slipback" is a major contributor to the achievement gap for low-income and minority children.[10]

• *Parent involvement:* All thirteen schools maintain active and multifaceted parent involvement programs, recognizing the importance of engaging parents at all levels and as early as possible. Parents are involved in helping to plan the community schools; they serve as volunteers or staff within the schools as members of parent leadership groups and as partners in their children's education. Parent coordinators work with DOE and CAS staff at each site to ensure that parents see the school as a place not just for children but for entire families.

• *Adult education:* Related to parent involvement is adult education, which consists of a wide variety of classes and workshops for adults, including other community residents, as well as parents. Common offerings are English as a Second Language classes, General Educational Development programs, adult basic education, and entrepreneurship and other employment-related programs. Some of the CAS community schools offer college courses in partnership with institutions of higher education.

• *Health services:* Five of the thirteen schools (three elementary and two intermediate) have medical clinics where students can receive their primary health care, as well as treatment for emergencies and illnesses. As a licensed health care provider, CAS operates its own clinics and regularly partners with area hospitals, including Mount Sinai and Columbia Presbyterian. In addition to having on-site clinics in five community schools, CAS offers medical services to three other community schools through a "school-linked" approach; students receive health care at the CAS Bronx Family Center, which is within walking distance of their schools.

• *Mental health services:* All of the CAS school-based and school-linked clinics offer extensive mental health services, including individual and family counseling, group therapy, in-depth assessments, referrals, and crisis intervention for students and their families. Clinicians (social workers with MSW or CSW credentials) generally have caseloads of eighteen to twenty-two students, with enough room in their schedules to see walk-ins and emergencies. In addition to providing clinical services, the CAS mental health staff provide classroom consultation with teachers and participate in schoolwide interventions designed to foster a positive school climate.

• *Social services:* Through its participation in the New York Times Neediest Cases campaign (an annual fundraising drive conducted by the newspaper to benefit seven New York City charities), CAS is able to provide financial assistance to families in need. Additional types of social services might include helping families locate housing, employment, or other needed resources.

• *Early childhood:* Two CAS community schools (P.S. 5 and P.S. 8 in Washington Heights) offer early childhood programs. Early Head Start is a "zero-to-three" program that works with pregnant mothers, helping them access prenatal care and learn about child development before and after their children are born, providing both home-based and school-based services. These children "graduate" into Head Start programs for four- and five-year-olds.

• *Community and economic development:* CAS community schools seek to become centers of their communities—neighborhood hubs that encourage lifelong learning and build social capital. To that end, CAS community schools regularly host community events and neighborhood celebrations (like the annual Dominican Heritage Celebration, which now draws hundreds of community residents); encourage adult political and civic activism (for example, by organizing trips for parents to participate in the annual After-School Advocacy Day in Albany, New York), and encourage student activism and community involvement. CAS fosters economic development at the neighborhood level by employing community residents in its partnership schools, supporting community businesses, partnering with financial institutions, and offering entrepreneurial classes for parents and other adults.

Staffing and professional development

Each CAS community school has a full-time director who works closely with the school's principal. Other key staff include a full-time program director (CAS staff member), an education coordinator (DOE employee who works part-time for CAS), and a parent coordinator (employed by CAS or by the DOE). At each site, the program staff is made up of teachers, youth workers, program specialists (such as dance teachers and artists), and high school and college students.

Professional development activities include orientation for new staff, monthly Community Schools Work Group meetings for site directors and other key staff, and workshops offered through CAS, Boys & Girls Clubs of America (of which CAS is a member), the Partnership for After School Education, and the After-School Corporation.

The role of the community school director is particularly central to the design and success of the model. The director serves as a two-way coordinator, linking the CAS services to those offered by the DOE and ensuring that the multiple services offered by CAS are connected to one another. This integrative role is perhaps the most important feature of the director's many responsibilities. Other major duties include developing and overseeing the site's budget, hiring and supervising staff, serving on key school committees (including the School Leadership Team, the Pupil Personnel Committee, and the Principal's Cabinet), and brokering additional services by partnering with outside organizations.

Partnership issues

CAS has learned the critical importance of nurturing relationships at all levels, including at the local schools, at the regions (which supervise the local schools), and at the citywide DOE. For CAS, the partnership with the New York City public schools is supported by a written agreement that was developed by CAS and the New York City Board of Education in 1990. This formal written agreement has been helpful throughout the many changes of administrations in the schools and in the city government throughout that period. Members of the CAS executive staff meet regularly with the leadership of the New York City schools, both to share information and to determine ways to deepen the partnership. CAS also nurtures the partnership by regularly holding dinner meetings with all of the community school principals and directors. These are occasions both for celebration and for joint problem solving.

Other implementation issues and lessons learned

CAS has learned many valuable lessons over the past thirteen years of implementing community schools in New York City. As our work has evolved, we have come to understand the critical role played by the community school director. Initially, CAS hired young and relatively inexperienced professionals (primarily social workers) for these positions, but we soon came to understand that the role is complex and that the requisite skill set is unlikely to be found in individuals with only a few years of professional experience; as a consequence, we have increased the salary range for these positions and recruited individuals with more experience in both programmatic and management arenas.

A related finding was that we needed to provide a wide range of support for our directors and other program staff; as a consequence, we have built an infrastructure that includes monthly role-alike meetings for key community school staff (directors, program directors, parent coordinators, office managers), a mentorship program for new community school directors, and a central staff that includes an education specialist and a budget director who provide program and fiscal support to the schools.

Research and evaluation to date

CAS has commissioned several external evaluations over the past thirteen years. The two initial CAS community schools—I.S. 218 and P.S. 5 in Washington Heights—were the focus of a six-year process and outcome evaluation conducted by researchers from Fordham University. The first three years primarily addressed formative issues; during the next three years, the evaluation addressed a variety of outcome issues, using a comparison design involving two other New York City public schools that were not community schools. Overall, key findings from these evaluations include improvements in attendance and academic achievement, increases in parental involvement, reductions in the number of suspensions, and improvements in students' attitudes toward school. Specifically, students at both P.S. 5 and I.S. 218 showed improvement in math and reading scores. This was true for students who graduated in 1997 and for a cohort that was followed between 1996 and 1999.

Finally, the Fordham researchers documented dramatic levels of parent involvement: 78 percent higher at P.S. 5 than at a comparable elementary school and 147 percent higher at I.S. 218 than at a comparable middle school. At the community schools, parents took more responsibility for their children's schoolwork, felt welcome, and were observed to be a presence in the schools more than in the comparison schools. Parents also received many social services, attended adult education workshops, and received medical services.[11]

A subsequent evaluation conducted by researchers from the Education Development Center examined the results of CAS's efforts to improve the quality of the after-school programs in five community schools that received funding through the federal 21st Century Community Learning Centers (21stCCLC) program. The researchers concluded the following:

[The] coordinated efforts of the district and CAS to focus on academic enrichment, raising standards and expectations for after-school staff and providing a literacy curriculum that combines rich, engaging activities with support for staff with a range of professional experience have all contributed to stronger partnerships and a more effective after-school staff with a shared sense of purpose. As a result, children and their parents see the after-school programs as safe places where participants can have fun and engage in activities that support their academic achievement.[12]

CAS is currently working with a team of evaluators from Act-Knowledge—an action-research firm housed at the City University of New York—to build on and add to these earlier findings through a "theory of action" approach that is examining if and how specific targeted outcomes are being achieved. One component of this comprehensive design focuses on six middle schools that have received funding through the New York State DOE's 21stCCLC program. This component is examining students' academic progress, attendance, and behavior through multiple measures that include school records (standardized test scores and report cards), as well as student and teacher surveys.

Cost and financing

For fiscal year 2004–5, the operating budget for CAS's thirteen community schools is approximately $14 million, which includes approximately $9.9 million for the extended-day, summer camp, teen, parent, and adult education components and $2.4 million for health services (medical, dental, and mental health). In addition, two sites have Early Head Start and Head Start programs operated by CAS; the costs for these programs are covered entirely by federal grants totaling approximately $1.5 million.

CAS generates support for its community schools through a wide variety of sources. During the initial years, core support came primarily from private sources, including foundations, corporations, and individuals, with the exception of health and mental health services, which are financed partially by Medicaid, as well as by other public and private sources. Our long-term strategy has been to move toward a solid mix of public and private funding for our overall services.

On the public side, CAS has received major support for our community schools through the 21stCCLC program (initially through a three-year federal grant made to Community School District 6 and subsequently through a five-year grant made directly to CAS by the New York State DOE). Other public sources include the New York State DOE's Extended-Day/Violence Prevention program and the State Office of Children and Family Services' Advantage After-School Program. In addition, on the public side, Medicaid partially supports our medical, dental, and mental health services. Another major funding source is the Soros Foundation's After-School Corporation program, which underwrites the after-school program in ten CAS community schools. This funding represents a mix of public and private dollars.

Aggressive private fundraising continues regularly. Community schools have turned out to be easy for donors to understand, and site visits to the schools have helped to translate their conceptual understanding into actual financial commitments. CAS has enjoyed steady financial support from a wide variety of foundations, corporations, and individuals on the private side.

Fees for services represent only a small portion of the income for our local community schools' work, but they account for approximately half the revenues for our national work.

Initially supported by a grant from the Carnegie Corporation of New York, the national adaptation work has enjoyed steady support from the Citigroup Foundation since 1999. This core funding helps to underwrite the thousands of site visits to our local schools and funds the advocacy efforts that have helped generate awareness of the CAS model and of the community school strategy more generally. Fee-for-service contracts underwrite training, technical assistance, and other kinds of consultations with schools, school districts, and community agencies around the United States and internationally.

Conclusion

The CAS approach to community schools is totally consistent with the theme of this volume of *New Directions for Youth Development*. CAS board and staff consider community schools to be a permanent line of work for the organization—one to which we are committed, regardless of the vagaries of funding. Although we work in partnership with others to generate stable and adequate financial support for community schools, we also regularly commit some of the agency's own resources to the work of community schools, recognizing that this work represents a powerful strategy for improving the lives of children and families.

Notes

1. Eccles, J. (1999). The development of children ages 6 to 14. *The future of children: When school is out, 9*(2), 30–44.

2. See, for example, Epstein, J. L. (1995, May). School, family, community partnerships: Caring for the children we share. *Phi Delta Kappan, 77*(9), 701–712; Henderson, A. T., & Berla, N. (1995). *A new generation of evidence: The family is critical to student achievement.* Washington, DC: Center for Law and Education.

3. Clark, R. M. (1988). *Critical factors in why disadvantaged children succeed or fail in school.* New York: Academy for Educational Development.

4. Vandell, D. L., & Shumow, L. (1999). After-school child care programs. *The future of children: When school is out, 9*(2), 64–80.

5. McLaughlin, M. W. (2000). *Community counts: How youth organizations matter for youth development.* Washington, DC: Public Education Network.

6. Benard, B. (1991). *Fostering resiliency in kids: Protective factors in the family, school and community.* Portland, OR: Northwest Regional Educational Laboratories, Western Regional Center for Drug-Free Schools and Communities.

7. Ianni, F. A. J. (1990). *The search for structure.* New York: Free Press.

8. Hodgkinson, H. L. (1989). *The same client: The demographics of education and service delivery systems.* Washington, DC: Institute for Educational Leadership.

9. Dryfoos, J. (1994). *Full-service schools: A revolution in health and social services for children, youth, and families.* San Francisco: Jossey-Bass.

10. Johns Hopkins University's Center for Summer Learning. (2004). *Research summary on summer programs.* Available at http://www. summer learning.org/resources/docs/Draft%20of%20Publication%20for%20Media%20Forum.pdf.

11. Brickman, E. (1996). *A formative evaluation of P.S. 5: A Children's Aid Society/Board of Education community school.* New York: Fordham University Graduate School of Social Services; Brickman, E., Cancelli, A., Sanchez, A., & Rivera, G. (1998). *The Children's Aid Society/Board of Education community schools: Second-year evaluation report.* New York: Fordham University Graduate School of Social Services and Graduate School of Education; Brickman, E., & Cancelli, A. (1997). *Washington Heights community schools evaluation: First year findings.* New York: Fordham University Graduate School of Social Services and Graduate School of Education; Cancelli, A., Brickman, E., Sanchez, A., & Rivera, G. (1999); *The Children's Aid Society/Board of Education community schools: Third-year evaluation report.* New York: Fordham University Graduate School of Education and Graduate School of Social Services; Robison, E. (1993). *An interim evaluative report concerning a collaboration between the Children's Aid Society, New York City Board of Education, community school District 6 and the I.S. 218 Salome Urena de Henriquez School.* New York: Fordham University Graduate School of Social Services.

12. Jeffers, L. (1999–2002). *Summary of key findings from the Education Development Center's evaluation of the District 6-CAS 21st Century Community Learning Centers Grant.*

JANE QUINN *is assistant executive director for community schools at the Children's Aid Society in New York City.*

In New York City and elsewhere, the experience of Beacons in developing learning environments that are both supportive and challenging is finding its way into public school settings, with promising results.

3

The New York City Beacons: Rebuilding communities of support in urban neighborhoods

Peter Kleinbard

"THE BEACONS are not just program, but really a system of neighborhood revitalization. They are part of the struggle of neighborhood residents to maintain and build community life. Many . . . have extended their work into the surrounding neighborhoods, working with local police precincts toward creating drug-free and violence-free zones."[1]

The first ten Beacons began operation in 1991 as a result of the recommendation of a commission appointed by then-mayor David N. Dinkins. Richard Murphy, commissioner of youth services, led the development and implementation. Michele Cahill served as a consultant in the design and created the Youth Development Institute (YDI) as part of the Fund for the City of New York, to continue support for the Beacons, as well as other youth development projects.

YDI provides technical assistance, training, and development opportunities for Beacons and their organizations. Thirty training

NEW DIRECTIONS FOR YOUTH DEVELOPMENT, NO. 107, FALL 2005 © WILEY PERIODICALS, INC.

events were conducted by YDI in the past year alone. YDI produces materials about youth development and fosters sharing and peer support through the peer technical assistance network.[2] YDI also raises private funding, which is re-granted to stimulate and enhance innovative programming by Beacons in areas such as youth development, literacy, community participation, and youth leadership.

Expansion

Beacons have expanded dramatically and are now operating in at least seven other cities, serving more than 200,000 children, youth, and families annually.[3] The expansion reflects the qualities of the model—its flexibility, appropriateness for young people and adults of different ages, and support for families. The Beacon framework is based on research findings and practitioner experience indicating that programs taking a youth development approach are more effective than those that focus on "fixing" specific youth problems or perceived weaknesses.[4]

Successful Beacon programs provide positive ways to meet youth needs for safety, a sense of belonging, and a feeling of mastery, as well as opportunities for young people to make decisions and contribute to others. The programs apply youth development principles in their activities, including:

- Caring relationships with adults
- High expectations for young people and adults who work with them
- Opportunities by young people to contribute or make a difference to others
- Activities that are designed to be engaging and interesting to youth
- Continuity in relationships

The New York City program

There are currently eighty Beacons in New York City. Based in local schools (primarily middle schools), the Beacons are operated by fifty-seven community-based organizations and serve 140,000 young people and families. Programs include after-school and evening activities such as homework and tutorial assistance; literacy programs and preventive services; General Educational Development, English as a Second Language, and computer courses, and recreational and cultural activities such as basketball leagues, arts and crafts, theater, and dance. Services are tailored by local organizations working with advisory panels to meet the needs of each community in which Beacons are located. Young people serve on these councils and have a major role in advising and working in programs.

The Beacons require extensive linkages with other local entities across disciplines in order to maximize resources and services to participating youth and adults. These include police precincts, community schools, planning boards and other community-based and governmental agencies, as well as religious and business organizations.

The New York City Department of Youth and Community Development (DYCD) funds community-based and other not-for-profit organizations so they can provide direct services in the Beacon school program. Each Beacon receives $400,000 per year, and $50,000 per year is provided to each site for school space-opening fees. In addition, through the YDI of the Fund for the City of New York, which serves as an intermediary organization that provides various kinds of technical assistance to the New York City Beacons, numerous private funders have committed more than $10 million to the Beacons for special programs, training, and evaluation. These include the Annie E. Casey Foundation, Open Society Institute, Pinkerton Foundation, Charles Hayden Foundation, and many others.

Beacon program examples: Literacy Peers and ComNET

Two exemplary Beacon programs are these:

• *Literacy Peers:* Saint Nicholas Neighborhood Development Corporation is a nonsectarian community development agency offering social services in the Williamsburg and Greenpoint neighborhoods of North Brooklyn. Founded in 1975 to improve housing conditions, St. Nick's opened a Beacon in Williamsburg in 1995, by way of providing more diverse services to neighborhood residents.

Through Literacy Peers, St. Nick's trains and supports adolescents in teaching elementary and middle school youth literacy skills at its Beacon. Youth trainees are taught the basics of literacy education and lesson planning; they also learn a range of exercises for improving vocabulary and reading comprehension. They learn classroom management and how to work with children with special needs. As a final class project, trainees plan an hour-long program centered on books they have selected. During the last two weeks of the class, students plan their individually designed literacy instruction and then take on regular teaching. Stipends are awarded to participants.

• *Computerized Neighborhood Environment Tracking (ComNET):* ComNET enables youth to improve their communities through a process of conducting street surveys, assessing the data they collect, and developing and presenting it to community leaders and government. Youth become change agents and advocates on behalf of their communities, improving the built environment and the quality of life in their neighborhood.

During the summer of 2004, youth participants in Beacons in three communities—Central Harlem, East New York, and Sunset Park in Brooklyn—identified street-level problems such as dangerously cracked sidewalks and roadways, graffiti, debris, dead rodents, and broken lampposts; they then recorded them using hand-held computers. During the seven-week pilot, 1,165 problems were recorded by these youth. They mastered a new vocabulary of street features and problems and learned how to operate hand-held computers with digital cameras. The young people sought to bring improvements in their neighborhoods. In one example, a dangerous condition—exposed wiring—was reported to New York City by a fifteen-year-old participant, and the condition was addressed within two hours.

Young people participated in meaningful roles in which they became knowledgeable, confident, and skilled at effective civic engagement. They learned and applied knowledge about how local government works and used technology to gather accurate data. They produced reports and presentations and participated in teamwork, map reading, and data analysis. The summer project is now being extended into the regular program year.

Evaluation of the Beacons

The Academy for Educational Development's School and Community Services (AED) has conducted a multiyear evaluation, with financial support from the Annie E. Casey Foundation. The two-phase effort has provided important knowledge, enabling the city's DYCD and YDI to shape both policy and technical assistance to practitioners.

The Phase I Evaluation looked at the initial implementation of the Beacons and reported the following:

- The centers are set up and operated in a way consistent with the core tenets of youth development practice, offering a wide range of activities that help youth develop positive behaviors.
- The Beacons offer an array of activities for adults, including educational and immigrant services, opportunities for volunteering, and employment and intergenerational activities.
- Each Beacon serves as a "safe haven" in the community, and sites have improved security in the area surrounding the school, serve as a base for community problem solving, engage local residents in community service, and host family and community events.

The Phase II Evaluation examined a variety of youth and community outcomes. It identified strengths of the initiative, as well as challenges that must be addressed. AED found that, first, the Beacons offer young people a place to develop and grow through challenging activities, caring relationships, and having opportunities to contribute to the Beacon and to their communities. Both surveys and interviews indicate that the majority of young people are taking advantage of these challenging activities and believe that they are developing new competencies because of their participation in the Beacons.

Second, the youth development quality of the Beacon environment and the activities offered to youth make a difference in their outcomes. Evaluators looked at both general and youth development quality. The former included safety, the organization of activities, consistent enforcement of the rules, and low youth-staff ratio. The latter included the five core elements of good youth development programming: opportunities for youth to (1) develop caring and trusting relationships, (2) participate in stimulating and engaging activities, (3) benefit from a continuity of adult support, (4) be challenged to grow through high expectations, and (5) connect with and contribute to their communities. In programs with higher youth development quality, young people were:

- More likely to feel better about themselves at the Beacon
- More likely to believe that youth of all races and ethnicities were valued at the Beacon
- More likely to perceive that staff had high expectations for their behavior and performance
- More likely to report that the Beacon helped them learn leadership skills
- Less likely to report that they had cut classes
- Less likely to report that they had hit someone to hurt them
- Less likely to report that they had stolen money or other property
- Less likely to report that they had gotten into a fight

The YDI has played an important role in conceptualizing and promoting high-quality youth development programming. Those sites with core staff most frequently attending YDI meetings and training activities had the highest-rated youth development quality and the most positive youth findings.

Among the challenges cited in the evaluation is the need to better develop opportunities for collaborations with schools and ensure that all Beacons have staff trained and capable of providing safe environments.

Replication and adaptation

There are two primary areas in which work from the Beacons is being adapted to other settings. First, many cities are drawing on New York City's experience to develop their own sites. Second, in New York City and elsewhere, the experience of Beacons in developing learning environments that are both supportive and challenging is finding its way into other settings, such as schools.

Beacons have been implemented in Chatham-Savannah (Georgia), Denver, Minneapolis, Oakland, Palm Beach (Florida), Philadelphia, and San Francisco. In each community, a local intermediary organization was created to support Beacon development. Each community has now developed several Beacons and has a local-capacity development organization to support them.

The most extensive evaluation of the adaptations has been Public/Private Ventures' study of the early implementation of the San Francisco Beacons Initiative.[5] The research team identified key accomplishments and challenges in early implementation. The study found that the new centers met most of their goals for implementation and programmatic diversity, as well as extensive community mobilization in support of the Beacons.

Through the new high school reform initiative in New York City and elsewhere, knowledge about youth development is being applied in the development of new high schools. Organizations that created and now operate Beacons are working with school-based educators to co-design and operate new, small high schools. Strategies such as those to sustain close relationships with adults, develop high expectations, and support youth leadership are at the center of many of these new schools. The involvement of Beacon organizations, as well as others with youth development experience, also provides capacity that augments the skills of teachers and other school-based staff. The application of youth development in urban high schools is an important and hopeful adaptation of youth development knowledge and experience in nonschool settings, especially in light of the persistent failure of high schools and the high percentage of students who are not able to complete; in New York

City only about 50 percent of students complete high school within four years.

Challenges

Beacons face challenges that are common to all out-of-school-time (OST) programs. Funding is a particularly difficult problem. As the demand for OST programs has grown, there has been a tendency to expand the number of programs but not to increase resources for each program. Many Beacons have been underfunded for years. They've been expected to serve more participants with the same funding they had when they opened. Similarly, expectations have changed and are more focused on academic impact, when few OST programs are designed or funded to get test results; rather, they provide a broad range of experiences that increase youth engagement in learning and family involvement. It is critically important that both funding and expectations be better aligned with the design and capacity of Beacons and other OST efforts.

Notes

1. Edelman, P. (2001). *Searching for America's heart.* Boston: Houghton Mifflin.

2. For a list of YDI publications, see fcny.org, under Strengthening Youth Development/publications.

3. Chatham-Savannah, GA; Denver, CO; Minneapolis, MN; Palm Beach County, FL; New York City; Oakland, CA; Philadelphia, PA; San Francisco, CA.

4. *Beacon profiles.* (2002). New York: Youth Development Institute.

5. *Working together to build Beacon centers in San Francisco.* (2001). Philadelphia: Public/Private Ventures.

PETER KLEINBARD *is director of the Youth Development Institute at the Fund for the City of New York.*

*Under the leadership of the University of Pennsyl-
vania's Center for Community Partnerships, the
university-assisted community school model is showing positive results for children and youth in West
Philadelphia.*

4

University-assisted community school program of West Philadelphia: Democratic partnerships that make a difference

Ira Harkavy

TRULY DEMOCRATIC PARTNERSHIPS between universities and schools
are a potentially powerful strategy for changing communities,
schools, and higher education itself. The partnerships described in
this chapter represent the fruits of two decades of collaboration
between the University of Pennsylvania (Penn), community organizations, and the public schools in Philadelphia (particularly
schools in West Philadelphia, where Penn is located). Penn's Center for Community Partnerships (CCP) has worked with other
neighborhood resources to create university-assisted community
schools that are centers of education and engagement and that provide a range of additional services for students, their parents, and
other community members. The specific partnerships described
here—the school-based community health promotion and disease
prevention program at Sayre Middle School and the literacy

NEW DIRECTIONS FOR YOUTH DEVELOPMENT, NO. 107, FALL 2005 © WILEY PERIODICALS, INC.

program at Drew Elementary School—offer insights into how the university and the community have worked together to create meaningful change.

The mediating structure for on-site delivery of academic resources is the West Philadelphia Improvement Corps (WEPIC)—a school-based revitalization program founded in 1985 whose central purpose is to produce university-assisted community schools that serve, educate, and activate members of the community. The West Philadelphia Partnership (WPP)—a community-based organization composed of institutions (including Penn), neighborhood organizations, and community leaders—coordinates WEPIC in conjunction with Penn and the School District of Philadelphia. Currently, over 150 courses at Penn are involved in these efforts, engaging more than 60 faculty members from diverse disciplines. More than 2,300 students are participating in academically based community service courses in the 2004–5 academic year. Penn students support all aspects of the WEPIC program by assisting in its evening, weekend, extended-day, and school-day programs.

Theoretical underpinnings of WEPIC

WEPIC is predicated on the notion that assisting struggling schools requires addressing larger community needs. School (and school system) change are inextricably linked to community change and community mobilization. Simply put, good schools require good neighborhoods. However, such broad-based action is possible only through democratic partnering.[1] School and community conditions are inextricably linked. However, this work must be an expression of the core educational mission of the school—teaching and learning—if it is to be sustained.

Schools, in addition to being key educational institutions, are an appropriate locus of community engagement because they *belong* to the community. They therefore have the capacity to be hubs of service delivery and community organization. For example, CCP's

Urban Nutrition Initiative works with local schools to help provide fresh produce to the community through its school-based fruit stand and gardening programs, studies issues of food security, and organizes community programs such as a fitness night and a farmers' market to help address the obesity crisis in the community. When schools fill this role, they can foster decentralized, democratic, community-based responses to significant community problems. Higher education institutions (and especially research universities) can be a source of support. However, because of their status as resource-rich and powerful local institutions (in many cities, institutions of higher learning are the largest private employer),[2] they also have the capacity to encourage systemic reform.

Commitment to democratic partnerships

Building democratic partnerships with local schools and communities is not easy and is not done quickly. In CCP's early years, Penn faculty and staff had to overcome community misgivings about Penn's motives. Years of neglect, as well as the negative consequences of campus expansion on the community, had created distrust of Penn. The challenge has been met one school and one neighborhood at a time, demonstrating Penn's long-term commitment to the partnership and to projects that are mutually beneficial.

Initial discussions at the school site always began with the principal (a school leader who is open to collaboration is key to effective partnership and provides the reassurance needed for teachers to participate). CCP staff were assigned to each school to understand its culture, work with teachers who were open to having Penn students and faculty in their classrooms, and help provide the Penn resources to develop community problem-solving activities and the associated curriculum that the teachers wanted to develop. CCP staff could then link academically based community service courses to the appropriate teachers and schools. Over time, thematic areas emerged that reflected the interests of school staff, as well as Penn faculty, and projects began to focus on issues such as community health and nutrition, community arts, literacy, and environmental health.

Example 1: The school-based Community Health Promotion and Disease Prevention program at Sayre Middle School

For the past twenty years, community leaders in West Philadelphia have pointed to the lack of accessible health care as a pressing problem. In the spring and summer of 2002, however, a group of undergraduates decided to do something about it. In their academically based community service seminar, the students focused their research and service on helping to solve the health care crisis in West Philadelphia. The students' research and work with the community led them to propose to community partners the establishment of a health promotion and disease prevention center at a public school in West Philadelphia—the Sayre Middle School.[3]

Students' research revealed that community-oriented primary-care projects frequently fail because of a paucity of adequate external funding. They rightly concluded that for a school-based community health care project to be sustained, it had to serve the curricular goals of both the public school system and the university. They proposed the creation of a health promotion–disease prevention center at a local school that would serve as a teaching and learning focus for medical, dental, nursing, arts and sciences, social work, education, fine arts, and business students. Community leaders found their proposal so compelling that it led to the development of a comprehensive school-based Community Health Promotion and Disease Prevention (CHPDP) program at Sayre Middle School.[4]

The program at Sayre Middle School was formally launched in January 2003.[5] The CHPDP program functions as the central component of a university-assisted community school, designed both to advance student learning and democratic development and to help strengthen families and institutions within the community. A community school is an ideal location for health care programs; it is not only where children learn but also where community members gather and participate in a variety of activities. Moreover, its multidisciplinary character enables the Sayre CHPDP program to be integrated into the curriculum and co-curriculum of both the public school and the university, ensuring an educational focus as well as sustainability for the Sayre Center. In fact, the core of the program is to integrate the activities of the Sayre Center with the educational programs and curricula at both Sayre Middle School and Penn. To that end, Penn faculty and students in medicine, nursing, dentistry, social work, arts and sciences, and fine arts, as well as other schools to a lesser extent, now work at Sayre through new and existing courses, internships, and research projects.

Health promotion and service activities are also integrated into the Sayre students' curriculum. Given this approach, Sayre students are not passive recipients of health information or health services. Instead, they are active deliverers of information and coordination and creative providers of service. In effect, Sayre students serve as agents of health care change in the Sayre neighborhood.

A considerable number and variety of Penn's academically based community service courses provide the resources and support that make it possible to operate, sustain, and develop the Sayre CHPDP program. Literally hundreds of Penn students (professional, graduate, and undergraduate) and dozens of faculty members from a wide range of Penn schools and departments work at Sayre. Because they are performing community service while engaged in academic research, teaching, and learning, they are simultaneously practicing their specialized skills and developing, to some extent at least, their moral and civic consciousness and democratic character. And because they are engaged in a highly integrated common project, they are also learning how to communicate, interact, and collaborate with each other in wholly unprecedented ways that have measurably broadened their academic horizons and demonstrated to them the real value of working to overcome disciplinary myopia.

Example 2: An elementary-level literacy program

Led by William Labov, professor of sociolinguistics and member of the National Academy of Sciences, the literacy program was initiated to address the persistent gap in reading achievement of minority students in the surrounding neighborhood. Drawing on his decades of research on African American vernacular English, Labov and his students created a program—the Individualized Reading Program (IRP)—that isolated each student's particular reading errors. They then developed a series of targeted reading materials that are not only linguistically appropriate for the students but are culturally engaging: the materials draw from the lives of West Philadelphia children and their neighborhoods.

The recognition that educators need to value where children are in their learning and the context of their lives has had measurable results in reading improvement. Drew Elementary School, for example, was the "most improved" on its reading scores statewide in 1999. The research has now expanded to include Latino youth in North Philadelphia, and Labov is working in several other cities with U.S. Department of Education and National Science Foundation funding. It is important to note that Penn students, as part of their linguistics study, played a key role in the program, including helping to create the overall framework, collecting the data necessary for reading-error diagnostics and community-based story narratives, and piloting and improving the curriculum.

The America Reads program

The CCP has helped recruit Penn work-study students and train them in Labov's methodology to serve as tutors for the program, working approximately ten hours per week each. In the first four years of the America Reads program at Penn, from 1997 to 2000, over 350 America Reads tutors worked in the West Philadelphia community to raise the reading levels of inner-city children. The IRP (1999) mentioned earlier, which was created in Penn's linguistics laboratory by Labov and Bettina Baker for use by America Reads tutors and teachers, was the main vehicle of instruction for the program. The graph in Figure 4.1 shows the results of a subsample of 114 children's progress after working with Penn tutors on three subtests of reading skills on the Woodcock Reading Mastery Tests-Revised. These subtests assessed word identification skills, decoding skills, and reading comprehension skills. Results indicate that the children served by Penn's America Reads program made significant increases in reading test scores.

When CCP began working with Drew in 1996–1997, the school was performing at the lowest possible level (1000) on Pennsylvania System of School Assessment (PSSA) reading and math exams. In 1998–1999, the school demonstrated the most dramatic PSSA increases of any school in the commonwealth. Since that time, the PSSA scores have been consistently higher than other schools in the area.

Figure 4.1. Pre- and post-tutoring national percentile scores on the WMRT-R subtests of Word ID, Word Attack, and Passage Comprehension

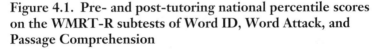

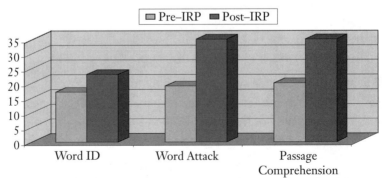

Source: Baker, Bettina. (1999). *Effects of a university-assisted community school based extended day program in literacy acquisition rates of inner city children.* Unpublished doctoral dissertation, University of Pennsylvania.

Another school with which CCP has been involved since 1995—University City High School (UCHS)—has experienced a dramatic improvement in a number of areas:

Graduation rates: There were 185 graduates in 1995, 240 in 1996, and 320 in 1997. Numbers since 1997 have held nearly constant, with some further gains recently.

Daily attendance: The rate for average daily attendance for the twenty-two comprehensive high schools citywide is approximately 65 percent. In 2000, UCHS had a schoolwide average daily attendance rate of 72 percent. During the 2002–3 academic year, the rate increased to 79 percent. The school-within-a-school most closely partnered with CCP had an average daily attendance rate of 87 percent in 2002–3.

Standardized test scores: UCHS's PSSA test scores increased in 1999, from the lowest possible scores of 1000 to 1050. The number of students scoring in the "Advanced and Proficient" category in reading more than doubled from 2001 to 2002, from 7.1 percent to 14.6 percent. The number of students scoring in the "Advanced and Proficient" category in math jumped dramatically between 2001 and 2002, from 1 percent to 15.2 percent.

Suspension rates: In comparison to the three other high schools in West/Southwest Philadelphia, UCHS has the lowest suspension rates.

Conclusion

The university-assisted community school model is showing results for children and youth in West Philadelphia. The preceding examples illustrate some of the ways in which Penn's CCP has coordinated universitywide efforts, in partnership with the community, in order to create and develop community school programs. The Sayre program, however, which is very much in its early days, is our most ambitious project. It aims to become a university-assisted community school, with a comprehensive community problem-solving curriculum and communitywide program that is fully integrated across both the Sayre curriculum and the curriculum of a number of Penn's schools.

The comprehensiveness and integrated nature of the Sayre program is attracting new partners and increasingly creative partnerships. The successful creation and operation of the Sayre CHPDP program strongly supports the validity of the basic proposition that *higher education can be a permanent anchor for revitalizing schools and communities if the vast resources it possesses, particularly its faculty, students, and staff, are brought to bear in a coordinated fashion.* The Penn-Sayre project, the Drew literacy program, and the University City High School results demonstrate that when universities such as Penn give very high priority to actively solving complex real-world problems in and with their local communities, a much greater likelihood exists that they will significantly advance the public good and realize their own potential.

Notes

1. Benson, L., & Harkavy, I. (2001, September). Leading the way to meaningful partnerships. *Principal leadership*, 54–58.

2. Harkavy, I., & Zuckerman, H. (1999). *Eds and meds: Cities' hidden assets.* Washington, DC: Brookings Institution.

3. Benson, L., Harkavy, I., & Hartley, M. (in press). Problem-solving service learning in university-assisted schools as one practical means to develop democratic schools, democratic universities, and a democratic good society. In T. Chambers, J. Burkhardt, & A. J. Kezar (Eds.), *Higher education for the public good: Emerging voices from a national movement.* San Francisco: Jossey-Bass.

4. One of the undergraduates who developed the Sayre project—Mei Elansary—received the 2003 Howard R. Swearer Student Humanitarian Award given by Campus Compact to students for outstanding public service.

5. Sayre is in transition to becoming a grades 9 to 12 high school and includes grades 8 to 10 in the 2004–5 academic year.

IRA HARKAVY *is associate vice president of the University of Pennsylvania and director of the Center for Community Partnerships.*

The public plays a critical role in establishing and sustaining full-service community schools.

5

Full-service community schools: Cause and outcome of public engagement

Richard Tagle

AS THE FEDERAL No Child Left Behind law places increased pressure on schools to improve the academic performance of all children—notably those who have been historically underserved—many educators are realizing that they cannot do the work alone. Now more than ever, the public schools need parents and other community leaders to work with them, not just to raise student test scores but, more important, to develop a community vision of successful, positive outcomes for children and youth. In response to this challenge, the Public Education Network (PEN) formed a Schools and Community Initiative, which involved local education funds (LEFs) in four communities across the country.

PEN is a national organization of LEFs and individuals working to improve public schools and build citizen support for quality public education in low-income communities across the nation. Its mission is to build public demand and mobilize resources for quality public education for all children through a national constituency of organizations and individuals. PEN and its ninety LEF members work in thirty-three states and the District of Columbia on behalf of 11.5 million children in more than 1,600 school districts, seeking

NEW DIRECTIONS FOR YOUTH DEVELOPMENT, NO. 107, FALL 2005 © WILEY PERIODICALS, INC.

to bring the community voice into the dialogue on quality public education in the firm belief that an active, vocal constituency will ensure every child, in every community, a quality public education.

PEN's Schools and Community Initiative, funded by the Annenberg Foundation, sought to address both the academic and nonacademic barriers to student learning and success by forging strong and deep relationships between public schools and other community-based programs and ensuring the provision of comprehensive supports for students. PEN wanted more than just to promote a community-school approach. It wanted to help communities better recognize the importance and the benefits of coming together—of engaging—around programs for young people. PEN believes that the more engaged the public is in the process of establishing and implementing full-service community schools, the more sustainable these community schools become.

PEN's public engagement framework: A theory of action

Undergirding the Schools and Community Initiative is PEN's framework for public engagement—a theory of action that includes a commitment to engage multiple constituencies, from opinion leaders and policymakers to the general, sometimes disenfranchised, public. PEN believes that when broad constituencies are engaged in the process of improving public schools, a stronger civic infrastructure is developed. Community members are able to see how their voices are heard, their opinions considered, and their time valued. Policymakers then begin to see an overwhelming constituency behind the issues and to act according to what their constituency is demanding. Thus the engagement process results in an increased local capacity to solve problems, a more vibrant economic life, and more citizens fully participating in a democratic society.

To understand this public engagement framework more clearly, PEN defines both the *public* and *engagement*. PEN defines *public* as three distinct audiences: (1) the *community-at-large*, (2) *organized stakeholder groups*, including sectors that have an interest in education that are formally organized to represent others and wield influence with policymakers, and (3) *policymakers* themselves.

These "publics" are engaged through a set of intertwined strategies: *community organizing, strategic planning,* and *advocacy.* LEFs work with partner organizations to advocate with local and state policymakers to address barriers to the effective implementation of local strategic plans or to take advantage of opportunities to accelerate their completion and effectiveness. LEFs in this case help identify the barriers and opportunities that become the fodder for state-level advocacy. They can also take positions on specific legislation or urge others with similar views to do the same.

By marrying this framework for public engagement with the model of full-service community schools, PEN believed it would establish long-term, sustainable linkages between public schools and their surrounding communities. They thought this would result in a deeper sense of responsibility for and ownership of public schools among community members, more local resources for community school efforts, and better policies to support and align with the community's goals and vision for its children and youth.

Implementing the theory

To test the theory, PEN provided $525,000 each to four LEFs that were selected through a competitive request for proposals (RFP) process, to spearhead communitywide planning and implementation efforts to establish, manage, and sustain full-service community schools in their school districts. These LEFs include the Lancaster Foundation for Educational Enrichment in Lancaster, Pennsylvania, the Foundation for Lincoln Public Schools in Lincoln, Nebraska, the Paterson Education Fund in Paterson, New Jersey, and the Education Partnership in Providence, Rhode Island.

Each of these LEFs established partnerships with their school districts, health and human service providers, community foundations, and other stakeholders to lead the community through a two-phase process. The first phase was a six-month planning process in which each LEF conducted a needs-and-assets assessment of the community. The LEF staff looked at health status, academic performance, supports and services available and accessed, and family situations. Information about the levels of collaboration, public and private resources that go into public schools, and challenges educators face in reaching academic goals and expectations was also analyzed. The LEFs presented their findings to their local partners and led the group into a strategic planning process addressing three key elements: (1) the services and supports that need to be made available and accessible, (2) resources and partnerships needed to put these into place, and (3) the advocacy needed to ensure that district and state policies are in place to support school-community collaboration.

Once the strategic plans were in place, the four communities entered into a three-year implementation phase in which the focus was on four key strategies: (1) putting the governance and administrative structures (including accountability systems) in place, (2) placing programs and supports in the public schools, (3) putting evaluation mechanisms in place, and (4) gearing up the partnerships that would help advocate for the needed resources and policies to help sustain all these structures.

In Lancaster, Pennsylvania, the Lancaster Foundation for Educational Enrichment (LFEE) and the Network for Safe and Healthy Children worked together to engage more than 120 community-based organizations to coordinate comprehensive supports and services for the school district's 11,400 students and their families. The LEF started out by establishing Family and Youth Resource Centers in three pilot elementary schools and addressed mental health and school safety issues identified by the community as priority needs for children and families. Within three years, these expanded into seven schools, with a plan to go districtwide with these resource centers and provide a whole array of supports and services for students, families, and the community-at-large.

In Lincoln, Nebraska, a local schools-and-community team, convened by the Foundation for Lincoln Public Schools, worked with the school district's 21st Century Community Learning Center Office to create the administrative structure that supported the establishment of fifteen community learning centers (CLCs) throughout the school district. These CLCs provide safe, supervised, cost-effective facilities for before- and after-school programs for school-age children, their families, and other neighborhood residents.

In Paterson, New Jersey, six elementary schools scheduled for renovation or construction are being designed as community schools, with space allotments for public use and health and social services. Community and state conferences were held by the Paterson Education Fund (PEF) to increase community awareness and understanding of the community school concept and its core framework and elements.

In Providence, a pilot program to turn an elementary school (in the poorest neighborhood of the city) into a full-service community school has been replicated to the feeder middle school. In 2004, the LEF received a grant from the Wallace Foundation to take their effort into a citywide program.

Key elements of effective implementation

The most important elements of effective implementation are these:

- *Strategic coordination:* Coordination in the four communities happened at two levels. Community school coordinators (or administrators) were placed in each of the schools LEFs worked with. In most instances, the LEF matched a service agency with a school, and the agency provided the in-school staff coordinator. These coordinators managed the various programs and supports within the schools, brokered needed resources with surrounding residents, businesses, and organizations, and facilitated interaction between and among educators, parents, and other community members. The second level of coordination was happening at the community level, with the LEFs or their appointed service agencies serving as key intermediaries between and among schools, service providers, municipal offices, and other local institutions. LEFs sought resources from community foundations and business entities, managed the governance and administrative structures, and convened community forums and partnership meetings to keep everyone informed and up-to-date about the initiative's progress.

• *Keeping the focus on outcomes for children:* A big challenge for these initiatives is the management of the various moving parts (from planning to implementation to evaluation to fundraising) being conducted by various players. Getting programs and supports into the schools where they are needed, involving the appropriate parties in key strategies, and putting structures in place are all well and good, but unless they lead to the desired outcomes for children and youth, these efforts are nothing more than mere ornaments. In Lancaster, Pennsylvania, for example, all programs and supports that are housed within the family and youth resource centers are aligned with the findings of the community assessment conducted by LFEE to ensure that students are provided with the prioritized supports needed.

• *Building and maintaining champions:* Even though a community has a common set of agreements regarding outcomes for children and youth and the use of full-service community schools as the primary strategy for attaining that vision, there still is a need to have a core group of individuals to serve as key advocates for the work to be done. Some key players may fall by the wayside and be pulled out by other concerns, funding may come in short, or differences in perspectives may cause partnerships to falter. LEFs in the four communities have served as champions for the vision—the strategies and the cause to keep the momentum of community action and collaboration going. In addition, LEFs sought the support of other key leaders in the community, including school superintendents, mayors, faith-based leaders, and business leaders. In Providence, for example, the Education Partnership had the support of Mayor David Cicilline, who used community schools as his campaign platform to get himself elected in 2003.

• *Addressing key policy issues:* The Paterson Education Fund in New Jersey focused on reform measures mandated by the State Supreme Court in a series of decisions based on *Abbott* v. *Burke*—a case filed by the state's Education Law Center in 1981. Recognizing that children who lack the basic necessities of food, health care, and family supports are at risk of academic failure, the court ordered the state to identify districts meeting a definition of "poorer urban districts" and to provide those districts with supplemental programs and services. Paterson is one of thirty New Jersey communities designated an "*Abbott*" district. In 1998, the court recognized that individual schools and districts also have the right to request on-site services, such as health and social service clinics, academic after-school and summer school programs, enhanced nutrition programs, and standards-based supplemental bilingual and special education programs. PEF saw an opportunity to make *Abbott* the platform for their Schools and Community Initiative and called for broad-based community engagement to ensure that new facilities built in Paterson will be community schools providing a full range of services. In 2004, the Paterson school board passed a bill requiring all public schools in the district to be community schools.

• *Holding partners and schools accountable:* When an initiative depends on the fulfillment of key benchmarks assigned to various agencies, the burden of holding these agencies accountable is situated in a trusted and respected entity. LEFs, due to their long-standing role in helping build school district and community capacities to improve schools, were in a unique position to do just that. By spearheading a strategic planning process in which goals, objectives, timetables, benchmarks, and resources were clearly laid out, LEFs were able to monitor the progress of both individual and collective activities of the partners. Agencies that faced difficulties in delivering a task tapped into the partnership for help. This way, the issues of turf and competition were minimized, and a sense of collective purpose and action began to form between schools and other community institutions.

Cost and financing

Each LEF received $25,000 for a six-month planning phase and $500,000 over a three-year implementation phase. Each LEF was also required to provide 25 percent cash and 25 percent in-kind match. Across all four communities, LEFs were able to raise more than $1.5 million in cash and in-kind matches, raising the total Schools and Community Initiative grant investment to $3.5 million.

These funds were used primarily to coordinate existing efforts, so minimum grant monies were spent on new services or programs. At the school level, LEFs linked with various existing programs to maximize the use of school space and staff. These community schools used the PEN grant to create an administrative structure, covering costs for coordinators, evaluation, and meetings. Supports and services were delivered through various programs such as a 21st Century Learning Community Centers grant, a Safe and Drug Free Schools grant, Title I funds, and contributions from local service providers, community foundations, and the private sector.

Evaluation and results to date

PEN developed a framework of potential community school and public responsibility outcomes that might be found in the participating sites. The framework differentiated among actors—policymakers (including mayors, city councils, school board members, and superintendents), organized groups, and the public at large—and stages of public responsibility outcomes, moving from simple attendance at events through voice, planning (including formal commitments), and, finally, action.

Outcomes were reasonably widespread among the sites. People convened by the LEF often adopt the vocabulary of the Schools and Community Initiative. When potentially adversarial groups emerge from a series of meetings with a shared way of talking about education, a LEF can reasonably claim to have made a difference in the voices that are speaking in the arena of public responsibility. Community awareness and knowledge about the definition of full-service community schools have been widespread in all sites. By bringing diverse groups to the table, some LEFs have broadened the local civic discourse, at least in the events that the LEFs themselves initiate.

Conclusion

LEFs are remaking their public schools into community hubs that serve students and adults alike. Academic instruction remains central, but students and teachers are supported by a multiplicity of other programs: after-school tutoring, mental health and medical services, social service programs for families (from housing to welfare), night school for adults (with classes on everything from English to job skills), and recreation and cultural services for everyone. This initiative was not only successful among the four LEFs that received the grant, but the lessons learned have been shared widely throughout the organization. PEN has become a member of the National Coalition for Community Schools, where its philosophy and experience can be imparted to other organizations.

By engaging broad constituencies across their communities, LEFs can not only establish needed programs and supports that help children and youth with their academic and social performance but can help create strong relationships between and among community institutions under a common vision. LEFs have become facilitators of schools and community; they bring the schools and the provider agencies together. By paving the way for

schools and community to be engaged in problem solving, strate-
gizing, and action taking, they facilitate the building of strong,
responsive full-service community schools that benefit not only students and surrounding neighborhoods but the entire community.

RICHARD TAGLE *is chief of staff at Public Education Network. He managed the Schools and Community Initiative from March 2001 through
March 2005.*

Chicago Public Schools, in partnership with the greater Chicago community, is implementing the largest-scale community school initiative in the nation. By bringing together public, private, and nonprofit entities, community schools in Chicago provide quality out-of-school-time activities and services that strive to improve the education, health, and wellness of students, families, and the community.

6

Anchors of the community: Community schools in Chicago

Elizabeth F. Swanson

Schools should be anchors of their communities, providing educational resources for the entire family. These are the guiding principles behind our Community Schools Initiative, which turns neighborhood schools into community learning centers that are open well into the evening hours—so they can provide educational and social-service programs, not just to the students, but also to their parents and other family members.

Mayor Richard M. Daley, January 28, 2003

CHICAGO IS the third-largest school district in the country, serving over 430,000 students in 602 schools. Chicago Public Schools (CPS) has a notable track record around educational reform initiatives, making an effort to involve city business leaders, as well as

NEW DIRECTIONS FOR YOUTH DEVELOPMENT, NO. 107, FALL 2005 © WILEY PERIODICALS, INC.

prominent community members, in strengthening the public school system. The establishment of Local School Councils (LSCs) and the creation of small schools, charter schools, and other alternative educational settings have propelled Chicago into the national spotlight. Chicago has truly become a laboratory for educational reform initiatives.

Arne Duncan, CPS's chief executive officer, and Mayor Daley have championed the Community Schools Initiative since its inception in 2002. Chicago's philanthropic community has also provided CPS with critical support. In fact, the Community Schools Initiative was developed in response to past success, as demonstrated by private foundations and their work with full-service neighborhood schools.

From 1996 to 2000, the Polk Bros. Foundation funded the Full Service Schools Initiative (FSSI) pilot project. Its purpose was to test a research-based framework for expanding school-based and school-linked services that would broaden support for children's well-being and school readiness and complement other CPS core strategies. The FSSI evaluation yielded four key findings:

1. Increased access to programs and services
2. Reduced mobility
3. Reduced truancy
4. Increased test scores

The success of FSSI, combined with additional philanthropic interest from Bank One and other local foundations, prompted the establishment of the Chicago Campaign to Expand Community Schools (the Campaign) in January 2002, which has brought together public and private agencies to support the expansion of community schools in Chicago.

The primary goal of the Campaign was to support the design and implementation of one hundred community schools in Chicago over the next five years (by 2007). The private partners participating in the Campaign, which now total seventeen entities, have been critical to the launch of the Community Schools Initiative and the success of this reform effort. Thus far, the primary focus of the private donors has been to provide seed grants to start new community school partnerships. However, as this initiative continues to grow, CPS will work with the Campaign to use private dollars more strategically in order to strengthen and sustain community schools in Chicago.

With the positive outcomes demonstrated by the participating FSSI schools, the local philanthropic commitment, and the mayor's backing, CPS was confident in launching the Community Schools Initiative.

Why community schools?

CPS places a high priority on providing quality after-school programs, particularly for underachieving students attending low-performing schools. Generally, these schools are located in communities characterized by multiple adverse systemic conditions, such as racial isolation, poverty, unemployment, crime, inadequate housing, and lack of public services. These adverse conditions tend to expose students to safety risks that place them in jeopardy and increase the likelihood that they will engage in risk-taking behaviors. CPS believes that after-school activities have the potential to act as buffers against these negative outcomes and are able to counteract the effects of a range of negative factors that contribute to students' lack of opportunities and underachievement. For children who face academic or behavior-related obstacles to success during the regular school day, the after-school hours can be a time to eliminate barriers and improve the education of the "whole child."

In 2002, under the leadership of Arne Duncan, CPS announced its aspiration to be the premier urban school district in the country and identified eight goals for the district in order to achieve that mission. Goal 5 specifies one key strategy as recognizing and strengthening schools as centers of communities in partnership with families. The district's plan goes on to identify the elements of effective schools and acknowledges the need for schools to function as "Community Schools" that employ comprehensive approaches for serving students, families, and community.[1]

Community Schools Initiative

In recent years, Chicago school reform has focused on the need to engage parents and the community in an effort to improve academic achievement and make it possible for schools to keep their buildings open after the regular school day. To date, sixty-seven Chicago public schools have become successful community schools through the Community Schools Initiative.

The CPS Community Schools Initiative includes two major programs: (1) the Chicago Campaign to Expand Community Schools and (2) the 21st Century Community Learning Centers. The mission of these programs is to foster the academic, social, and emotional support needed to ensure that all students succeed; they achieve this by offering activities before, during, and after the school day for students and their families. Activities are designed to support the school's academic program and expand the services offered within the community. Programs offered at each school vary, evolving in response to identified needs among students and the community, but most community schools in Chicago offer some combination of academic enrichment activities for students, adult education and English as a Second Language classes, student and adult technology training, art activities, recreation, and health services.

Program model

Similar to many other successful programs mentioned in this issue, the CPS initiative requires that, in order to be selected to participate, each school must appoint a full-time coordinator and establish an advisory group. Unique to Chicago, however, is that each CPS community school must also do the following:

- *Partner with at least one nonprofit organization (NPO):* CPS asks that community schools partner with NPOs that have a minimum of three years experience implementing after-school programs or a demonstrated track record of providing successful educational and related activities that enhance the academic performance and positive development of CPS students. NPOs must also demonstrate a history of collaborative leadership and willingness to work in true partnership with the school's principal, personnel, and parents. NPOs are critical to the success of this initiative, as they bring additional expertise and resources to Chicago schools and communities. The need for after-school programs, as well as health and social services, is great within the CPS population, and the public schools cannot possibly address all these needs on their own. By collaborating with local nonprofit agencies, community schools are able to meet the needs of more children and promote healthy development, using a more holistic approach to educating children.
- *Ensure that all out-of-school-time programs relate to and support the school's academic program:* The after-school programs that are offered at community schools are typically a combination of academic and enrichment activities. Whether a school is running a culinary course, creating a school newspaper, or offering an arts integration activity, the programs intentionally include both academic and social outcomes. Community schools are encouraged to offer a minimum of twelve hours of after-school activities per week, including parent programming. Most CPS community schools have programming until 5:00 or 6:00 P.M., including health and social services, and many have Saturday and summer program offerings.

In addition to these requirements, principal leadership is also factored into the selection process. Principal leadership is critical to the success of the community school, as schools often experience a true "culture change" as they implement the community school framework. In order to effectively implement and sustain the core principles, a principal must embrace collaborative leadership, have the ability to create and maintain partnerships, communicate effectively with both staff and community, and embrace those values embodied within the idea of community schools.

Resources and sustainability

The various funding streams that support the Community Schools Initiative, including the private contributions managed by the Campaign, total $12 million. CPS contributes $10 million, which includes local funding and funds garnered through competitive grants, and the Campaign has raised over $2 million in additional private money to support the initiative. However, CPS's commitment to students during their out-of-school time does not rely solely on the community school model and associated funds. The CPS Office of After School and Community School Programs coordinates and supports a variety of after-school activities. CPS is currently funding programs that serve over 200,000 children (about 46 percent of the student population). This is well beyond what comparable large urban areas are providing during the out-of-school hours (New York currently serves about 26.7 percent of their students, and Los Angeles serves about 12.9 percent).[2]

The Office of After School and Community School Programs currently funds five major out-of-school-time programs, in addition to the Community Schools Initiative. Sites that operate the after-school reading and math program called After School Counts receive an average of $30,000 to provide services; schools with the federal Supplemental Educational Services (SES) tutoring program receive an average of $150,000 to offer reading and math programs after school.[3] CPS offers an additional $15,000 enrichment grant for schools to provide programming beyond their academic offerings. Finally, sixty-one schools receive an additional $10,400 to run the After-School All-Stars program—a comprehensive after-school program that combines academics, recreation, and health and life skills.

Funding provided to schools through the Office of After School and Community School Programs is often based on formulas that include student population, which means some schools receive upwards of $600,000 in funds to support out-of-school-time programs. As noted earlier, in addition to CPS's existing after-school programs, the district, in partnership with the Campaign, provides approximately $130,000 per school in additional funding for the community schools. This extra support allows schools to provide programs and resources above and beyond academic after-school programs, as well as programs that already exist at the school.

The bulk of after-school and community school funding comes from CPS but is supplemented by grants generated by the Office of After School and Community School Programs and the Campaign to support activities such as family literacy, the provision of social services, and health and wellness programs. For example, a partnership with the Chicago Department of Public Health (CDPH) and Oral Health America (OHA), with support from Ronald McDonald Charities and the Michael Reese Health Trust, offers prevention-oriented dental health services for all second- and sixth-graders at CPS community schools. Another partnership with the Illinois Hunger Coalition (IHC) and the RealBenefits program helps community school students and families apply for income-support programs such as food stamps, medical programs like Kid-Care/FamilyCare, and cash assistance. In addition to supplemental grants, schools are also offered support for professional development and evaluation, thus promoting long-term sustainability.

As part of CPS's commitment to high-quality programming and sustainability, community school principals, resource coordinators, teachers, and social workers are provided with a variety of professional development opportunities. The Campaign provides the primary leadership for the community schools' technical assistance (TA) plan through the use of six "core" TA providers and four "niche" providers. The role of the core providers includes helping sites embrace the holistic nature of community schools, developing the four principles of the community school model, and establishing the necessary processes and infrastructure to implement and sustain the four principles. During the 2004–5 school year, the TA strategy was expanded to include four niche providers that provide expertise on specific programs or practices such as parental engagement, services to non-English speaking students and families, and data-driven decision making. In sum, community schools receive initial and ongoing assistance through these external organizations, with each school receiving a minimum of four hours technical assistance each month. These sessions are designed to keep principals, resource coordinators, and nonprofit partners working together to create and sustain unique programming for their students.

In addition, all new sites receive training in the nuances of running a community school. Resource coordinators, principals, and nonprofit partners are brought together to share best practices and are provided an opportunity to work together in creating a service plan that works for all participants. CPS also provides schools with an after-school manual that outlines programming, best practices, job descriptions, and various methods for improving after-school programming. In addition, the CPS Office of Specialized Services will soon be releasing a "Coordinated School Health Program" manual to the community schools (and eventually districtwide), which is designed to help schools address the complex health issues that exist within our schools and communities.

In the past year, CPS and the Campaign have further extended their commitment to the community school model and its continued success by partnering with the University of Chicago, School of Social Service Administration (SSA). The new Community Schools Program at SSA is a partnership that will serve to sustain community schools in the coming years. SSA provides a theoretical and research-based framework that serves to bolster current professional development offerings to partners within the CPS Community Schools Initiative. In addition, the program will provide schools with a highly trained pool of leaders who will have the tools to run effective programming following the community school model.

As the community school movement continues to grow and develop in Chicago, it is important to consider sustainability efforts.

CPS has committed to expanding the model to one hundred schools by 2007 (growing from the current sixty-seven), promising to sustain schools with additional funding well into the future. These schools have devoted resources and personnel to the idea of full-service institutions—those that will serve students, parents, and the community as a whole. CPS is committed to servicing and sustaining these vital urban community-learning centers.

Accomplishments and results

CPS's commitment to community schools is clear. The district has worked hard to craft and attain a broad vision for after-school and community school programs, which includes providing comprehensive programs for students in out-of-school time and incorporates needed programs and services for parents and community members. The CPS Community Schools Initiative has also leveraged a number of new resources, which have dramatically increased the programs and services offered to students and their families. Thirty-four lead nonprofit partners have been secured for the schools, including the Boys & Girls Clubs of Chicago, Children's Home and Aid Society of Illinois, and Metropolitan Family Services. These partners bring specific expertise, including youth development and social services, as well as technical assistance capacity, that are best suited to meet student needs; such expertise includes tutoring, mentoring, instructing in culinary and fine arts, counseling, and encouraging healthy living. In addition to the lead partners, over three hundred additional community partnerships, which include one-day events such as health fairs and violence-prevention workshops, have been instituted.

CPS programs and reform efforts are currently evaluated by academic outcomes and test scores. Although community schools should (and will) be evaluated on a variety of indicators (including academic and social indicators), the CPS Community Schools Initiative is proving to have a positive impact on student achievement.

In 2003–4, 70 percent of community schools demonstrated gains on the reading portion of the Iowa Test of Basic Skills. In addition, 76 percent of the 21stCCLC demonstrated gains on the Illinois Student Achievement Test. Although these indicators alone do not prove success for our community schools, they do signify that our students are benefiting from the community school effort, and academic achievement is on the rise.

As the Community Schools Initiative continues to expand to one hundred schools, CPS recognizes the need for continued quality, both in our programming and in our staffing. Professional development will continue to be a large part of our effort to ensure excellence, as will ongoing evaluation efforts. If this program is to succeed for students, parents, and their communities, CPS must also maintain quality partnerships, both with the Chicago philanthropic community and in our community neighborhoods. These are vital next steps in ensuring that each school is truly an anchor of its community.

Notes

1. *Every child, every school: An education plan for the Chicago public schools.* September 2002.

2. Interviews with district personnel.

3. SES is a component of Title I of the Elementary and Secondary Education Act, as reauthorized by the No Child Left Behind Act, which provides additional academic instruction, specifically reading and math, outside the regular school day. SES is provided by both CPS and private tutorial companies (approved by the Illinois State Board of Education). The average cost per student, if enrolled in a private program, is $1,200. As a result, the average school budget for SES is far greater than other after-school programs provided by the district or nonprofit organizations.

ELIZABETH F. SWANSON *is the director of After School and Community School Programs for Chicago Public Schools.*

A model of community-school partnerships is developing in a school district in Evansville, Indiana.

7

The School Community Council: Creating an environment for student success

Daniel Diehl, Cathy Gray, Ginny O'Connor

THE FIRST FULL-SERVICE school in Evansville, Indiana, began at Cedar Hall Elementary School in the mid-1990s. The principal— a former kindergarten teacher at the school—recognized that children were coming to school unprepared to learn, mostly as a result of issues originating outside school. She applied for funding, and in 1989 a large grant came through the United Way of Southwestern Indiana from the Indiana-based pharmaceutical firm Eli Lilly that allowed youth service agencies to collaborate with the school to provide after-school programming. In 1994, another grant enabled the school to develop a community outreach program that helped at-risk children and families in the community access human services in a more coordinated way. Given their successes, the Cedar Hall Elementary School principal was approached by the United Way to develop a pilot site.

In the planning phase of the Cedar Hall pilot, the United Way brought in Jody Kretzman to share a model for mapping community assets.[1] By way of promoting children's school success, a number of community-based organizations, businesses, parents, and churches were invited to come together to explore solutions. This

NEW DIRECTIONS FOR YOUTH DEVELOPMENT, NO. 107, FALL 2005 © WILEY PERIODICALS, INC.

meeting led to the development of a school site council and marked the beginning step in viewing problems facing the school as community issues. Next, a plan of action was developed, based on a full-service school (FSS) framework. Joy Dryfoos, who had just published her first book on community schools, was contacted.[2] She advised the staff to visit other national models, in varying stages of development.

As a result, the site council agreed that the model for Cedar Hall's FSS should consist of the following components: (1) family literacy provided through the school's Family Resource Center and Even Start program; (2) health services provided by a local hospital's mobile outreach clinics, the school nurse, and the public health nurse; (3) social services provided by local mental health agencies, case managers, and school social workers; (4) parent involvement through special-events programming; (5) after-school and summer programming through community agencies and school staff, and (6) the curriculum defined according to Indiana's state educational standards.

The neighborhood became organized into an active association that worked with the school to meet the needs of the surrounding community, resulting in decreased crime rates and a cleaner, friendlier, and healthier environment. Ultimately, the results included improved grades, improved discipline, and improved physical and dental health of the neighborhood children.

Recognizing the success of the model, the superintendent appointed the school principal as supervisor and encouraged the expansion of the model throughout the district. In 2000, a district council was created—the School Community Council (SCC)—and in 2001, a grant from the Welborn Foundation—a local health foundation—supported the expansion of the full-service model through the SCC. An infrastructure of support was developed, and a project director, assistant director, and administrator were hired. Every other month, all partners meet to hear about the work of the various teams and share information; a steering committee meets monthly to support the work of the SSC and various other subcommittees, such as a health committee, a programs and services committee, an after-school committee, a communication committee, a site council support team, and an evaluation committee.

Core components: The practice

Several components drive the success of the SCC:

- *Infrastructure and organization that allow for growth:* The SCC assists community agencies and schools in understanding the policies and procedures related to providing programs or services and shares minutes from meetings with all collaborative partners and, by doing so, builds strong relationships, which are critical to the practice's success.

- *Ownership in the process:* The SCC tries to create an environment where community partners feel as though they are part of the decision-making process. For schools, this involves principal leadership, as well as support of faculty and staff. The principal is responsible for everything that happens within the building and is viewed as the gatekeeper of all programs and services. This frame of reference allows the principal to determine the degree of involvement in the process. Faculty and staff also must have buy-in for the process to be successful.

- *Relationships built on trust:* Prior to the birth of SCC, Evansville schools could be traditionally called closed and self-contained systems. With the many demands, significant responsibility placed on safeguarding students, and constant scrutiny of public schools, their normal reaction was to protect students and guard against outside political agendas. However, the SCC has created a process whereby partnerships can be explored and trusting relationships can be established. This mutual trust is paramount if true collaboration is to take place.

- *Bottom-up, not top-down process:* To ensure that programs and services are responsive to the needs of students and families, all programs and services delivered through the SCC are directly related to the issues identified by school site councils.

- *Evaluation along the way and not at the end of the road:* Evaluation of the SCC is an ongoing process. It is designed specifically to measure the effectiveness of implementation strategies and provide ongoing feedback regarding the progress toward objectives. Because this is a developing model, ongoing evaluation allows for adjustments in the model's implementation.

- *Use of coordinators:* Through grant funding, the SCC has provided some part- and full-time site coordinators to orchestrate the delivery of programs and services in schools. Principals hail these positions as instrumental in promoting access to services at schools. The coordinators work with community partners to provide programs in the school, and provide organization to the school site councils. They record data vital to the evaluation of programs and services, and they work as a team to explore ways to improve programs and services for students. Given the demands on the school principal, these positions provide support for the additional work associated with full-service schools.

Experience with implementation

It is apparent in doing this work that not every principal in every building understands what we are trying to do. The decades-old traditions and structures of public schools do not necessarily lend themselves to system changes that threaten controls. Even with the schools doing this work, there are continuous challenges and obstacles to overcome. We have learned that this is an ongoing process that needs support and nurturing every step of the way.

Our schools, principals, and staff are overwhelmed in this climate of accountability and consumed with trying to do a job that asks more of them and yet provides them with fewer funds. At the same time, they are trying to deal with children coming to school often less than ready to learn. A few small steps at a time are sometimes the best we can do. We are not trying to force something new on people who simply cannot deal with it. Instead, we offer to help in small ways to foster relationship building between schools and their communities. Small steps make a big difference in creating trusting, lasting partnerships, and long-term change. Here are a few examples:

- A local hospital that closed had wheelchairs, beds, furniture, and all manner of equipment our nurses could use in the various buildings. The SCC worked to bring those goods to those schools in need.
- Partnerships were formed with another hospital to bring their professional employees into schools to give wellness training for staff, students, and parents, to support exercise programs, to serve as dieticians and respiratory therapists, and to work at in-school health fairs.
- A grocery store manager attends a school site council meeting and provides a hospital dietician with free ingredients for her classes in schools and frequent gift certificates for the school to get fresh fruit to sell as snacks or for rewards for various activities.
- Later, when that school's students decide to participate in a Walk for Juvenile Diabetes because of a recently diagnosed classmate, the grocery store provides free bananas for the students, the PTA provides water, a group of local university students provide music and fun, and members of the SCC participate in the walk as well.

Cost and financing

Because of strong community collaboration, the Evansville-Vanderburgh School Corporation (E-VSC) has been able to obtain two federal 21st Century Community Learning Center grants for seven elementary schools and three middle schools. A grant received from the Indiana Department of Education will provide three years of technical assistance to the corporation to develop a coordinated school health plan. Coordinated school health is a way of improving children's health and removing barriers to learning. It focuses not only on health and physical education but includes other components needed to help schools become healthy, including comprehensive school health education, physical education, counseling,

psychological and social services, family and community involvement, nutrition services, school health services, healthy school environment, and school-site health promotions for staff. This funding
should greatly aid our efforts going forward with the full-service
school concept and model. However, sustaining this initiative continues to be a challenge. Dollars are scarce. This work requires careful management and coordination of existing resources and a keen
eye for being able to identify grants that fit with the mission.

Research and evaluation

Evaluation of the SCC is an ongoing process that is conducted
internally and externally. Under the direction of the SCC steering
committee, the evaluation committee identifies and tracks key indicators of success in an effort to continuously improve the collaborative process. The committee has recently completed a three-year
evaluation report summarizing progress toward stated objectives.[3]
Key outcomes related to specific goal areas follow:

• *Development of an infrastructure of support and strong collaboration:* An infrastructure has been developed, and the E-VSC has
reorganized the administrative structure to support the process of
school-community collaboration. Partners have developed a shared
vision involving the collaborative identification of goals and objectives. A number of funding sources have been obtained and leveraged to support the work of the SCC.

• *Physical health:* High immunization rates (over 98 percent) are
being maintained, as well as high percentages of students receiving
physicals (over 70 percent for kindergarten and sixth grade). This
is credited to collaborative partnerships between school nurses, local
hospitals, and the local health department. Further, there is evidence of an increasing percentage of students having access to dental services through a Mobile Outreach Clinic, as well as increases
in the availability of health-related programs focusing on nutrition

and fitness. Despite these positive outcomes, approximately 37 percent of elementary and middle school students were identified as overweight or at risk for becoming overweight. Although this represents a snapshot in time, it underscores the importance of providing additional health-related programs in schools.

• *Mental and emotional health:* Students referred for school social work services have shown improvements in family functioning and overall school adjustment. These services were shown to have immediate effects after only one month and sustained effects at three- and six-month intervals.[4] Further, there has been a decline in students using drugs, alcohol, and tobacco on a monthly basis, as well as declines in binge drinking. Also there is evidence of improvement in the early identification of and early intervention with students having mental health, behavioral, and drug and alcohol problems, as well as increases in the number of prevention and early-intervention programs provided for youth and families. Despite these findings, suspensions show mixed results. While the majority of the targeted schools have shown fewer suspensions, other schools have high rates.

• *School readiness and adjustment:* Over the past four years, the percentage of students served in after-school and summer programs increased, as did the number of days students were attending. Students attending over thirty days in after-school and summer programs show higher reading and math grades, fewer regular school-day absences, and overall behavioral improvements, as reported by teachers, compared to student attending no programs or fewer days.[5] Attendance rates in targeted schools have improved, with the greatest changes occurring in the last three years. E-VSC continues to maintain higher graduation rates than the state average.

Evansville is a place that has embraced the concepts of full-service community schooling. The level of involvement by all sectors of the community is encouraging. Schools have benefited in a variety of ways, and the results are beginning to show up, both in child health and academic achievement.

Notes

1. Kretzman, J., & McKnight, J. (1993). *Building communities from the inside out: A path towards finding and mobilizing a community's assets.* Chicago: Acta Publications.

2. Dryfoos, J. (1994). *Full-service schools: A revolution in health and social services for children, youth, and families.* San Francisco: Jossey-Bass.

3. School Community Council Evaluation Committee. (2004). *School Community Council evaluation summary.* Available by request: Dan Diehl, Evansville-Vanderburgh School Corporation, 1 SE 9th Street, Evansville, IN 47708.

4. Diehl, D. (2003). *Social work services in schools: Evaluation of a school community social model.* Unpublished doctoral dissertation, University of Louisville.

5. School Community Council Evaluation Committee. (2004).

DAN DIEHL *is director of the Evansville-Vanderburgh School Corporation, 21st Century Community Learning Centers, and chair of the School Community Council evaluation committee.*

CATHY GRAY *is assistant superintendent of federal projects for the Evansville-Vanderburgh School Corporation, director of the School Community Council, and a former elementary principal.*

GINNY O'CONNOR *is a registered nurse, assistant director of the School Community Council, and chair of the Nutrition and Physical Activities Team.*

How can a city, without a large infusion of new dollars, craft systemic strategies to increase the number, impact, and sustainability of its full-service schools? A new approach in Boston shows signs of success.

8

Aligning systems to create full-service schools: The Boston experience, so far

Andrew L. Bundy

IN AUGUST 2000, twenty people met in a room in Boston to address two questions: (1) How can Boston create a network of community schools? (2) Does the action have to proceed one school at a time, or are there systemic changes that can advance the movement?[1] Those were hard questions.

In the room were the leaders of the half-dozen different full-service school initiatives then under way in Boston. In the prior decade, Boston's full-service schools had produced well-documented improvements in child, family, and school outcomes. These leaders knew, as subsequent research has strongly confirmed, that many of the barriers to school success are not academic, but social and economic.[2]

Special thanks to Joy Dryfoos, Lainy Fersh, Marta Gredler, Karen Hansen, Nechama Katz, Bill Kelley, Susan Klaw, Matt LiPuma, Jane Quinn, Kathleen Traphagen, and Margot Welch.

NEW DIRECTIONS FOR YOUTH DEVELOPMENT, NO. 107, FALL 2005 © WILEY PERIODICALS, INC.

They also knew from personal experience that serious problems in vision, leadership, and service delivery were not limited to the public schools but were commonplace throughout the human services sector. They believed that parents and families needed a larger role. They were convinced that full-service schools, with their twin focus on children, parents, and communities and on student achievement, were the most promising way to reform *both* human services *and* public education. Though proud of their achievements, they were frustrated by the pace of change. Most important, they knew that the next stage of the work had to be systemic: a one-school-at-a-time approach was leaving too many children and communities behind.

For the next four years, a core team of these leaders worked together, without funding, a road map, or recognition, to figure out how to spread full-service schools across the city. By 2004, they had earned the support of Mayor Thomas Menino and Superintendent Tom Payzant, received start-up funding, and become a thriving coalition of public agencies, schools, and community organizations.

The organization they created is called the Full-Service Schools Roundtable (FSR). Its mission is to advance the academic success and healthy development of students in Boston through integrated school-community partnerships. A core goal of FSR is to foster a realignment of public resources and an expansion of private resources to be integrated and directed toward full-service schools.

FSR must focus on systems and resources already in place and ask questions—common to most communities—that zero in on "systems change opportunities." How can Boston better align the work of schools, human service organizations, families, and neighborhoods across entire communities? What obstacles to school-community collaboration must be overcome? How does Boston develop the public will to invest in and sustain large-scale changes in its systems of care and education, with a rigorous focus on results?

Starting up the Roundtable: 2000–2004

Superintendent Tom Payzant sparked the formation of the Round-table. Responding to a question from author and full-service school advocate Joy Dryfoos at a Harvard conference on full-service schools in March 2000, Payzant observed, "Full-service schools are great, but how do you make them grow across a school system? How do you begin to reach many schools, not just a few? Show me a way to make full-service schools systemic. When you can do that, we can go to work."

The effect of this challenge on Boston's organizers of full-service schooling was galvanizing. Within months, the first gathering of Boston's full-service school leaders was held, drawing people from five nonprofits, two universities, three city agencies, a local consulting firm, and the school department. A team from the Coalition for Community Schools facilitated a series of meetings to help the group frame its thinking and develop an initial plan.

Core challenges quickly emerged. The city lacked any coherent vision for community or full-service schooling. Public funding was rigidly divided into inflexible funding categories. Private funding, although sometimes generous, was finite and contested. Although there was much talk about fragmentation of services, participants could cite few existing strategies to counteract the problem. Worst of all, in 2000 the country and the region were entering a frightening economic downturn.

In addition to external, contextual challenges, the emerging group had its own conflicts and issues. First, they were collaborating with competitors. These program administrators—the architects of full-service schooling in Boston—were routinely engaged in hardscrabble competition with one another for foundation, corporate, and public sector dollars. Second, there was no money to support this systemic, citywide organizing work; the first four years of the Roundtable's work took place through in-kind help, on borrowed time. Finally, none of the institutions for which these individuals worked was *primarily* committed to full-service schools; their organizational missions were in public education, health, mental health, human services, children's advocacy, or higher education.

What FSR looks like now

In the spring of 2005, a full-time executive director leads a small team of consultants and graduate students.[3] A volunteer steering committee, made up of leaders of FSS efforts across the city, serves as a policy-setting body. Three workgroups of Roundtable members focus on managing data and information, providing technical assistance, and developing financing strategies.

Although FSR is organized and governed as an independent public-private partnership, it is housed in the Unified Student Services offices of Boston Public Schools (BPS), where the district's many community-partnership, health and human services activities are coordinated citywide. This "independent co-location" is a deliberate strategy to preserve the independence and flexibility of the coalition while deeply partnering with the public schools, as a system.

Lessons learned

The Roundtable has learned several lessons that may be of use to other communities:

- *Embrace a mission, not a model.* Perhaps the most important early decision the FSR partners made was to advance a strategic approach—the school-based alignment and coordination of human services and public education to support positive student outcomes in learning and development—rather than a specific program model. Working in this way, FSR can:

Target systems rather than programs
Encourage a wide range of schools, partners, and models

Engage in multiple emerging ventures, across many disciplines
and systems

Avoid being bound by prescriptive approaches of single institutions
or leaders

• *Enlarge the vision to align the work of many, overcoming "the silo
effect."* FSR's membership is up to seventy institutions and individuals, and climbing. Much of its work counteracts the "silo effect"
of vertically organized, noncooperating systems of care and education. FSR brings together principals and BPS administrators, health
and mental health providers, faith-based organizations, business
leaders, youth development and after-school leaders, funders, and
city and state agency staff. This strategic integration of the work
spans disciplines and hierarchies, improves communication, and
fosters partnership.

• *Build relationships based on trust and a willingness to take risks.*
The principles for building the Roundtable are the same as those
for creating a full-service school. A full-service school can only
become "the real thing" when the collaborators have tested
and strengthened their bonds by meeting and overcoming
challenges and problems. The same notions of trust building, working hard, and collective risk taking apply in the growth of the
Roundtable.

• *Target multiple systems.* Many people in the full-service school
movement, including myself, have made the mistake of thinking
that public school systems must be the main, or exclusive, focus of
system reform. FSR understands, from long experience, that effective full-service school work is about *accessing, reforming, and
realigning multiple systems of care and education to improve outcomes for
children.* In its first year of staffed activity, FSR has launched projects with leading elements of the city's health care, after-school,
mental health, community center, youth development, higher education, philanthropic, and nonprofit human services communities,
as well as the Boston Public Schools.

• *Practice strategic opportunism: Choose a few projects for maximum,
leveraged impact.* FSR chooses its initiatives carefully, seeking

maximum impact through "leveraged" opportunities that are enhanced by the work of others. In each instance, the creative work of others is magnified and extended by FSR.

• *Plan for and take advantage of leadership changes.* Most setbacks in full-service schooling in Boston involve changes in leadership. Paradoxically, great successes also come from transitions. Full-service school advocates have convinced new agency heads to serve as champions. An incoming leader with a mandate for change tackles and resolves problems that a previous administration recognized but could not address.

• *Do not depend entirely on leaders at the top; people in the middle can do a lot.* Virtually without exception, the leaders of FSR have been senior program staff, faculty, and administrators of both public and private entities rather than superintendents, CEOs, executive directors, mayors, or deans. What FSR has lacked in executive capacity (like the ability to spend discretionary resources or to make faster decisions), it has made up for in quality project design, the creation of a sustainable effort, time to work out problems, and tangible results. Top leaders, of course, are indispensable, and in Boston they have been highly effective. But FSR's success comes, in part, from top leaders' support of the people who do the daily work.

• *Persist, persist, persist!* It took four years of behind-the-scenes organizing to launch the Roundtable. A core team carried on through years of cuts, survived intense rivalries, and weathered the inevitable practical and philosophical disagreements. Participants focused on transforming the Roundtable from a planning enterprise to an active series of initiatives to promote system change.

The challenges ahead

Several major challenges must be met if FSR is to achieve its ambitious goals:

• *Build the public will to invest.* The full-service school movement is reliant on soft money, both public and private. Prominent regional campaigns to create full-service schools are driven by large, unsustainable philanthropic investment. San Francisco, Multnomah County, Oregon, and New York City boast heartening examples of publicly funded, sustainable full-service school initiatives, from which Boston and the nation must learn.

- *Widen the circle.* Although proud of the inclusiveness and transparency of its work, the Roundtable has work to do to engage the diversity of the city. Those not sufficiently represented include health care providers, labor, community action agencies, state agencies, parent-led organizations, faith-based organizations, elected officials, higher education, and older youth, among others.

- *Hold one another accountable for child and youth outcomes, across systems.* FSR's members must generate more and better evidence of their impact if they are to prevail in the policy arena. Human services agencies must be able to show that their full-service school activity results in improved child health, mental health, or other outcomes. Schools must post better academic results and link them to their full-service school interventions. All full-service school partners must share one another's missions: schools will succeed when their human service agency partners succeed, and vice versa.

- *Become expressly political.* In Massachusetts, advocates for early childhood, child health care, and after-school have increased public investments in these fields. For FSR to follow in their footsteps, it must become more political. FSR needs working alliances with constituency-driven organizations that share its vision and can mobilize legislative and political action.

- *Worry less about finding new money and more about spending existing funds well.*

The right questions

The systemic expansion of full-service schooling—and the success of all our children—depends on a large-scale public reimagining of the role of schools and human services in our society. Can a citywide network of full-service schools be created? Will it increase children's success? How can Boston create the alignment of existing systems necessary? Can one city or state forge the public will to effect major funding and policy changes? How? These hard questions are the right ones. It is a measure of FSR's impact that many more Boston leaders are beginning to ask them. The real test of the Roundtable is to begin to provide some answers.

Notes

1. May 31, 2000, memorandum from Joy Dryfoos to Tom Payzant. The terms *community school* and *full-service school* are used interchangeably to describe a school that is open after school and partnered with nonschool organizations, providing student and family support (in academics, after-school, family literacy, mental health counseling, parent leadership and engagement, health services, or case management), and deliberately addressing the nonacademic barriers to student learning. FSR believes such schools develop along a continuum. Phase 1 schools have a minimum of one university or community-based organization (CBO) partner; Phase 2 schools have a full-time site coordinator and one or more programs in the areas listed; Phase 3 schools have multiple programs; and Phase 4 schools boast a formal partnership with a CBO with a written Memorandum of Agreement, partnerships with at least one additional university or CBO, a shared governance structure that includes the school, the lead CBO, and parents, and extensive programming.

2. Rothstein, R. (2004). *Class and schools: Using social, economic, and educational reform to close the black-white achievement gap.* New York: Economic Policy Institute and Teachers College Press.

3. For more information on the Roundtable, contact Marta Gredler, executive director, Full-Service Schools Roundtable, c/o Unified Student Services, Boston Public Schools, 443 Warren Street, Dorchester, MA 02121; 617–635–6537; mgredler@boston.k12.ma.us.

ANDREW L. BUNDY *is a principal of Community Matters, a research and consulting firm, and he serves on the steering committee of the Full-Service Schools Roundtable.*

Through Schools Uniting Neighborhoods, county and city, school and community developed a unique collaboration to support fifty-one community schools.

9

Schools Uniting Neighborhoods: The SUN Initiative in Portland, Oregon

Dianne Iverson

THE DECISION of the City of Portland and Multnomah County to partner together to support schools in a more comprehensive community school model occurred in 1998, under the leadership of former Multnomah County chair Beverly Stein, city commissioners Jim Francesconi and Dan Saltzman, and then-county commissioner Diane Linn. They were seeking to improve the way resources for students and their families were delivered by developing a school-based and school-linked delivery model. While staff researched models across the country, elected officials cultivated support from their colleagues on the city and county commissions and in key departments.

This initiative was possible because of many years of collaboration between county and city departments and individual schools. Some of our schools had school-based health clinics, some had community schools, some had alcohol and drug counselors, and some had personal relationships with area nonprofits. What occurred in the next few years was a definition of a system of care for school-age youth that used the school as an organizing principle for services and made services equitable throughout the entire county.

NEW DIRECTIONS FOR YOUTH DEVELOPMENT, NO. 107, FALL 2005 © WILEY PERIODICALS, INC.

In the spring of 2003, elected officials decided to carry the collaboration even further by folding all services for school-age youth and their families, including SUN Community Schools and the Bureau of Parks and Recreation's Community Schools, into a single full-service package as the anchor of a School-Age Policy Framework for Multnomah County. The School-Age Policy Framework uses a school-based delivery model to bring a core set of services to high-need schools.

The SUN Community School model

The SUN Community Schools Initiative is a community-driven model that allows each school community to design the programs that fit neighborhood needs, while working toward core goals that stretch across all SUN Community Schools. The common goals are as follows:

- To increase the capacity of local schools to provide a safe, supervised, and positive environment for expanded experiences that improve student achievement, attendance, behavior, and other skills for healthy development and academic success
- To increase family involvement in a child's education, as well as support the school and school-based activities that build individual and community assets
- To increase community and business involvement in supporting schools and school-based programs that combine academics, recreation, and social-health services
- To improve the system of collaboration among school districts, local governments, community-based agencies, families, citizens, and business and corporate leaders
- To improve the use of public facilities and services by locating services in the community-based neighborhood schools

SUN Community Schools tailor their programs, events, and services to the neighborhoods they serve, based on local needs assessments. An advisory committee at each school brings together school staff, parents, community leaders, students, and partner agencies to determine the best ways to support youth and families. Because they are locally driven, each SUN Community School looks different. Some partners and activities are at every SUN Community School, and some are unique to a single site. However, there are three main components of the model, which can be thought of as the three legs of a stool, each necessary to maintain the balance and effectiveness of the whole: (1) academics, (2) social and health services, and (3) extended-day activities.

A nonprofit lead agency such as Metropolitan Family Services serves as the managing partner for each SUN Community School, bringing social service expertise, knowledge of the community, and additional resources to the school. Lead agency staff work with the principal and advisory committee to select a site manager. The SUN Community School site manager coordinates extended-day programs, links SUN activities to the academic school day, fosters strong relationships with school personnel and community partners, and identifies networks of services, programs, and resources that can benefit youth and the larger community. The City Parks and Recreation Bureau oversees twelve SUN Community School sites, which are staffed by city employees.

Core components

SUN Community Schools differ according to the particular needs and resources in the area, with a mix of on-site services and community-based services to which children and families are referred:

- *On site:* Manager or coordinator, twenty hours of extended-day programming a week for children, family outreach and engagement activities, case manager for children and their families
- *On site or in the community:* Early childhood services, access to culturally specific services, health services, library services
- *In the community:* Antipoverty services, mental health services, assessment services, sexual minority and gender-specific services

Experience with implementation

SUN Community Schools started in 1999 as a pilot project, with eight schools and $1 million in funds. The project was primarily focused on extended-day programming, family involvement, and community and business involvement. We recognized early on that schools should not be chosen solely by the superintendent with a mandate that they become a community school.

Over time, schools have been selected in a variety of ways to partner with the city and county. During the pilot phase of SUN Community Schools, a key component in the initial selection process for choosing schools included an application process to show that a particular school had enough leadership assets to make it a collaborative community school and not just a place that shared a facility. Parents, youths, and educators at a school joined in the application process and were required to sign off. After the written application was submitted, each school participated in a ninety-minute interview with the selection committee. Youth, parents, and educators were encouraged to be part of the interview team for each site.

Selected school-community partnerships are awarded a core service package equivalent to $120,000 worth of resources. As of 2005, $16.7 million from the county's Department of School and Community Partnerships is now focused and aligned around a *full-service community school model*, with school-based and school-linked services in fifty-one sites. Linkages to a variety of services from early childhood prevention services to high-risk antipoverty services are coordinated or provided by the same agency that provides the school-based services. The county aligned existing resources instead of finding new resources to fund this system of care for school-aged children and families.

Lessons learned

With seven years of experience, we have learned quite a lot about the pleasure and pain that goes with collaboration:

- *Use coordinators.* Site managers need a strong mix of people skills and planning skills. They also need the capacity to run a complex program while being accountable to multiple entities, including the school, the sponsoring nonprofit lead agency, and the county Department of School and Community Partnerships.

- *Principals should be champions.* There is no substitute for well-informed and committed leadership at each site. In recognition of that reality, the involvement of the school principal in SUN is a critical factor in whether or not a school is chosen as a SUN Community School site. One challenge is that principals sometimes transfer to another school, and the incoming principal may not have the same level of commitment to SUN. In the event of a change in principal, a thorough orientation to the SUN vision is required, helping the new principal clarify what role he or she wants to take with the SUN Community School.

- *Establish common vision and goals.* Early on, SUN Community Schools Initiative staff realized that without a clear vision and goals, it was difficult to get partners, school staff, and community members to buy into the SUN Community School concept. Using a group process to create the vision and goals gives people an opportunity to come together as a team, get to know each others' strengths and prioritize areas of interest, and identify emerging leaders who have a strong commitment to the SUN Community School.

- *Balance initiative-wide consistency with site autonomy.* Having a common vision and goals at the initiative-wide level facilitates planning, evaluation, and technical assistance for the SUN Community Schools as a group. The challenge is to design a system with enough flexibility for individual schools to tailor activities to local needs and interest. For example, the initiative has an overarching goal of increasing family involvement, but that goal is met in different ways from school to school. Each site needs to best support its specific community.

- *Create systems of communication at every level.* The best way to ensure that the program keeps running smoothly is to keep the lines of communication open. SUN Community School Initiative staff found it especially useful to work with school principals and lead agencies to clarify roles and responsibilities so that each could provide appropriate support to the on-site managers and leadership for the initiative.

Evaluation

The original evaluation of SUN Community Schools measured academic performance, family involvement, community and business involvement, and volunteerism, as well as the numbers of students participating in programming. During the first year of operation, SUN Community Schools saw academic performance increase in reading and math in the elementary schools targeted. It took three years to see similar results in the middle schools targeted.

During the 2003–4 school year, academic performance continued to improve, both schoolwide and with targeted students attending more than thirty days during the school year. The partnership was able to show not only whole-school performance trends but trends of students who have been participating in enrolled activities on a regular basis. The performance measured is based on meeting state benchmarks in reading and math. Data are collected and analyzed for each of the SUN Community Schools.

SUN Community Schools is looking for a national partner to assist them in the cost of designing a long-term evaluation based on the data already gathered. An extensive baseline evaluation, as well as a Year One follow-up, can and will be used as a starting point for a longer-term evaluation of individual student performance. The county is pursuing outside resources to assist in this more extensive long-term evaluation of the initiative.

Future financing

On the broader political scene, the level of support for education and children's issues in the city and county has been remarkable. In response to economic and social service crises, elected officials, school district employees, and the community at large worked collaboratively throughout the school year to pass three levies to restore and expand funding for vital services. The levies included a City Parks levy, a City Children's Initiative, and a temporary county income tax primarily for school funding, for total yearly revenue of over $130 million dedicated to education and children's services. Key political leaders promoted these three levies, and the community has supported them.

The SUN Community Schools Initiative in Multnomah County, Oregon, is funded through a variety of sources, the county being the single largest donor. Some $16.7 million worth of resources in one county department (the Department of School and Community Partnerships) are aligned around a common vision and goals: student success. The second-largest donor of funds is the City of Portland's Parks and Recreation Bureau.

The last five new SUN Community School sites have been funded through grants from the state and through a local children's initiative sponsored by Portland city commissioner Dan Saltzman. Even in this tight economy, the prognosis for Portland's SUN Community Schools Initiative is optimistic. Most people in our community support its existence, and most schools would like to be selected to participate.

DIANNE IVERSON *is the education policy director of chair Diane Linn's office in Multnomah County, Oregon.*

*Positive results from one of California's most success-
ful education mandates—SB620 1991, or Healthy
Start—are chronicled from around the state.*

10

California's Healthy Start:
A solid platform for promoting
youth development

Lisa R. Villarreal

A PIONEER EFFORT when passed as a bipartisan bill into legislation
in 1991, California's Healthy Start initiative now stands out as a
promising model for the emerging community school movement.
Healthy Start is intended to bring "comprehensive, integrated, supports and services" to California's most disadvantaged K–12 students and schools. Building on the theory that student development
and learning are deeply disrupted by barriers such as hunger, ill-
ness, unemployment, illiteracy, violence, trauma, and the cycle of
poverty, the Healthy Start authors sought to seed a system that
offered the opportunity and funding to initiate partnerships to help
reduce barriers to learning and promote positive outcomes for the
neediest students.[1]

Healthy Start grants create the capacity for students and parents
to be leaders and decision makers in their communities. They help
schools and other child- and family-serving agencies to reorganize,
streamline, and integrate their programs to provide more logical
and effective support to children and their families. They do this
by insisting on plans that foster systemic change.

NEW DIRECTIONS FOR YOUTH DEVELOPMENT, NO. 107, FALL 2005 © WILEY PERIODICALS, INC.

To obtain Healthy Start funding, collaborative teams of school and district personnel, in partnership with community agencies and organizations, are required to submit competitive grant applications to the California Department of Education (CDE). Applicants must document their intentions to develop, integrate, and sustain support services and opportunities that will reduce the barriers to learning in their school communities. Applications must demonstrate evidence of an authentic community assessment, integration with the academic goals and school improvement plans, and plans for sustainability beyond the grant cycle.

Applicant schools must also demonstrate need by verifying that no fewer than 50 percent of their students are eligible for the state Medicaid program, qualify for free or reduced-price lunches, or be English-language learners. Grants are monitored by the California Department of Education, through mandatory annual budget and evaluation reports. Recognizing the need to provide unencumbered access to support and resources to bolster the success of these local grants, grantees are also provided with training and technical assistance by CDE and, for the past thirteen years, the Healthy Start field office, located at the University of California at Davis.

Other funding streams can be used to supplement Healthy Start grants. For example, sites can be reimbursed for select certificated services provided by school psychologists, speech and hearing therapists, school nurses, and other Medicaid-approved providers. These reimbursements, as well as reimbursements made available by the state for selected Medicaid administrative activities, can contribute significantly to the sustainability of a site.

Core components

Since a local collaborative group determines the partnerships and the design based on their unique community assessments, programs are different at each Healthy Start site.

Site-specific programming

Sites and their programs evolve according to local needs, strengths, geography, partners, and diversity. If vandalism and graffiti and its resulting legal problems are a barrier to learning, the Healthy Start site might engage arts and recreation partners to bring after-school programs that will promote positive artistic expression and a performing stage for those who were formerly making a canvas of freeway overpasses and fences. If random youth violence is identified as a barrier, the collaborative will probably select academic, youth development, counseling, and law enforcement partners to create programs that offer positive alternatives to violence. If, however, community violence is seen as an issue of economic desperation, the collaborative may also partner with economic development programs to provide positive adult education, employment training, and opportunities for youth and their families.

Attendance problems can also be a challenge to student academic achievement. Some sites have discovered that many of their tardy or absent students care for younger siblings in the morning when the parents have already gone to work, so those sites work to implement alternative day-care partnerships for youngsters before and after school. But other sites find that their student absences are due to a sheer lack of public transportation at appropriate school hours, so they will attack the problem in a different way, engaging civic transportation partners.

Some sites in the coldest mountain regions of California have high absence rates in the winter because the children simply do not have proper jackets and boots to wear to school in the snow; "good parents" would never send their children out to freeze. These sites conduct a lot of clothing drives to reduce their barriers to learning. It is regrettable that some sites have parents whose lives are so consumed with drugs and drama that they don't bother with their children in the morning. Joan Reynolds of the Lake County Office of Education talks about a five-year-old who got up, dressed, and crossed a major highway alone every morning while his drug-dealing parents slept. His Healthy Start site had breakfast, a toothbrush, hair comb, jacket, and a big hug waiting for him every day.

Although the unique attributes of Healthy Start sites may differ, the necessary elements they address for creating a positive learning environment are constant. These elements include:

- Creating emotional and physical safety nets at school and in the community
- Building relationships among students, teachers, parents, providers, the school, and the community
- Providing guidance and emotional support for academics and life issues
- Offering practical support for basic needs
- Deepening child, youth, and family knowledge of what it means to be young and developing in a challenging world

As Healthy Start sites evolve, so does their depth of youth and family involvement in the community, as evidenced by the following examples.

Maria Velasquez, of Newman Healthy Start in San Joaquin, talks about using the "neighbors-helping-neighbors" model to train parents to do outreach to other parents in their communities. Parents who began as clients of her clinics and centers are now providing instructional aid in the classrooms and supervision on the playground at recess; they also serve on the school site councils. Their models of "one-stop" family resource centers earned them a U.S. Department of Agriculture award of achievement in community economic development, which has attracted other funders to support their work.

Naya Bloom, of Los Angeles, talks about the cross-pollination of programs that all began with a Healthy Start grant. Students have created "Peace Games" and an annual Health and Peace Family Festival. There is a "Promotora" program of parent and community advocacy, an Obesity Task Force, an Asthma Coalition, and substantial sharing of resources. These programs are growing roots into the community that will still be strong long after the initial grant funding is over.

Use of coordinators

Each Healthy Start operational grant features some kind of coordinator at the site, district, or even county level. Coordinators maintain the collaborative by planning meetings, delegating and supervising providers, designing and integrating the programs within the school improvement plan, and attending school, district, and county meetings. Some even provide case management to their families, although coordinators seem to function best if they do not act as direct service providers but do have experience in the field of education, health, human service, or recreation, or with one of the lead partner agencies.

These dedicated leaders wrestle with issues such as the joint supervision of workers (who may come from various agencies and be trained in various disciplines) and establishing and maintaining working agreements around confidentiality, information sharing, school integration, joint use of facilities, and liability. Coordinators do everything from designing working spaces to attending the highest-level city and county meetings to nurturing key partnerships. An astute coordinator, with the support of his or her collaborative, must also carefully create marketing messages to leverage their results into long-term commitments for ongoing relationships.

Partnerships

The California Healthy Start model is built on cooperation, coordination, and collaboration.[2] Collaborations must be win-win situations for all parties involved. This is the only way for an initiative to work with little or no funding actually changing hands. Issues of shared staff, shared facilities, shared supervision, or shared leadership, governance, oversight, and decision making all come into play, particularly for the site coordinator. Budget crises can also create scenarios in which partners are tempted to retreat to traditional, stand-alone service systems. Collaborative partnerships are difficult to maintain because they require constant attention to ongoing relationships and agreements. But because their mission is to serve the same student population, successful collaboratives ideally enable the partnering agencies to sustain their partnership with the school site long after the grant period ends.

Sustainability

Healthy Start sites are intended to continue beyond the funding cycle. The sustainability rate of California's Healthy Start sites went from about 90 percent in the first five years to about 75 percent after thirteen years, according to a study from UCLA conducted by the CDE.[3] There is no renewal option for the Healthy Start state funding based on daily attendance or any other quantifiable measurement available to Healthy Start grantees, so sites must rely on the contributions of their collaborative, public and private grants, and other philanthropy and partnerships to survive. Sustainability also hinges on the site's ability to involve youth and community, sustain a coordinator, and partner with key organizations for fiscal agency and access to philanthropy.[4] Many advocates argue annually that positive evaluation findings such as the ones that follow warrant a serious conversation about the state's obligation to continue funding the initiative.

Research and evaluation to date

Healthy Start works; it has undergone several impressive statewide evaluations since its inception. The first, conducted by SRI International in 1995, revealed significant gains in child well-being, family functioning, and quality of life but very small gains in academic achievement.[5] The second evaluation, conducted by CDE in 1998, revealed nearly identical results as the 1995 SRI evaluation but featured new gains in academic achievement for the lowest-performing students. Families reported a 50 percent reduction in use of hospital emergency rooms for nonemergency health care; they also reported a 50 percent reduction in the incidence of family violence and depression. Sites noted a 12 percent decrease in transiency and mobility rates; schools reported a 40 percent increase in parental involvement, and families reported a 6 percent increase in employment rates. The Department of Education took a close look at academic achievement by isolating the bottom quartile (25th percentile and below) of student achievement. They noted a 25 percent increase in reading scores and a 50 percent increase in math scores for the lowest-performing elementary students.[6] Since those first two evaluations, CDE has contracted with Sacramento State University to write an updated version of the statewide evaluation guidebook. Reports as recent as 2003 continue to reveal nearly identical results to the first two evaluations.

The bottom line is that Healthy Start works by not only "raising the bottom of academic achievement" for California's lowest-performing students but also by making a significant contribution to the quality of life for individual children, neighborhoods, and communities.

Political history of Healthy Start

Many state and federal initiatives have been modeled after the California Healthy Start legislation. State leaders of other collaborative initiatives confirm that "most successful partnership programs in California now have Healthy Start in their genealogy."[7] Collaborative innovations, however, are always subject to the politics and political will of the public and their elected officials. Enormous budget deficits across California and the nation have taken the spotlight off comprehensive student and family supports and services and placed it more singularly on targeted services such as after-school programming. The California legislature and past two governors have consistently reduced the once-robust Healthy Start funding (of $19 to $39 million annually through 1998). Although after-school programming is absolutely essential to the success of K–12 public schools and may be the most important public school initiative of the decade, after-school programming represents only a portion of what is done in a successful Healthy Start site. Yet today, both Healthy Start and after-school providers will tell you that it is going to take both initiatives to successfully create the essential building blocks for learning and to set the stage for positive youth development.

The future of Healthy Start

Newer initiatives have come along since Healthy Start was initiated, each containing some of the elements of the Healthy Start approach. The California After-School Initiative passed in 1998 and the "After School for All" (Proposition 49), passed in 2003, are both examples. These initiatives hold some promise to provide renewable funding sources for desperately needed after-school programs across the state, starting with the neediest schools. These programs, bolstered by 21st Century Community Learning Center funding, will go a long way to sustain the tutoring, arts, recreation, enrichment, service learning, and business partnerships that are so key to positive youth development.

Neither piece of legislation, however, contains the comprehensive array of supports, services, and opportunities for children, youth, and their families contained in Healthy Start. Maintaining the building blocks for a positive learning environment to develop positive youth development practices remains a challenge when the counseling, health and human services, basic needs, and parent involvement pieces are not included in new initiatives. So our mission continues: to promote the comprehensive components and broader partnerships of a Healthy Start approach into new initiatives for children, youth, and families.

Notes

1. Adelman, H., & Taylor, L. (2004). *Guidelines for a student support component.* Los Angeles: University of California, Los Angeles, School of Mental Health.

2. Healthy Start Field Office. (2001). *Collaboration module: A guide to authentic partnerships and real change.* Davis: University of California, Davis.

3. UCLA Center for Healthier Children, Families and Communities. (2001). *The Healthy Start Initiative in California: Final report.* Los Angeles: University of California, Los Angeles.

4. Jehl, J., Blank, M. J., & McCloud, B. (2001). *Education and community building.* Washington, DC: Institute for Educational Leadership.

5. Wagner, M., & Golan, S. (1996). *California's Healthy Start School-Linked Services Initiative: Summary of evaluation findings.* Menlo Park, CA: SRI International.

6. California Department of Education. (1999). *Healthy Start works: A statewide profile of Healthy Start sites.* Sacramento, CA.

7. Villarreal, L., & Bookmyer, J. (2004). Community-school partnerships: The living legacy of Healthy Start. In *What works policy brief.* Sacramento: Foundation Consortium for California's Children and Youth.

LISA R. VILLARREAL *is executive director for the Center for Collaborative Research and Educational Supports and Services, University of California, Davis, and vice chair for the National Coalition for Community Schools.*

Moving the community school agenda forward requires leadership with a clear vision, a focus on results, and the community capacity to bring schools to life and sustain them.

11

Building the community school movement: Vision, organization, and leadership

Marty Blank

A COMMUNITY SCHOOL is more than a traditional school. It is a set of deliberately formed partnerships that provide the supports and opportunities that are important to students, families, and the surrounding community. Community partners can include health and social service agencies, family support groups, institutions of higher education, youth development organizations, government, community groups, or others—all organized around a common goal: to create the conditions necessary for all children to learn at their best. Here are the conditions:

1. The school has a core instructional program with qualified teachers, a challenging curriculum, and high standards and expectations for students.
2. Students are motivated and engaged in learning, both in school and in community settings, during and after school.

NEW DIRECTIONS FOR YOUTH DEVELOPMENT, NO. 107, FALL 2005 © WILEY PERIODICALS, INC.

3. The basic physical, mental, and emotional health needs of young people and their families are recognized and addressed.

4. There is mutual respect and effective collaboration among parents, families, and school staff.

5. Community engagement, together with school efforts, promotes a school climate that is safe, supportive, and respectful and that connects students to a broader learning community.[1]

The assumption behind education reform today seems to be that only the first condition—quality instruction and teaching—matters. For all our children to succeed—particularly the most disadvantaged—advocates of community schools argue that all these conditions must be met.

Because they work to link school and community resources and to integrate what happens academically with what is happening in the lives of students as a purposeful part of their design and operation, community schools have the following three major advantages that schools acting alone do not:

1. *They garner additional resources for the school and reduce demands on school staff.* Community schools reach outside their walls to leverage services and programs that help meet a range of needs that affect student learning, including family mobility, violence, unsupervised out-of-school time, and other issues that have become facts of life for too many children in today's society. This approach gives principals and teachers more time to concentrate on their core mission: improving student learning.

2. *They provide learning opportunities that develop both academic and nonacademic competencies.* Community schools support the intellectual, physical, emotional, social, and civic development of young people. Consistent with the principles of youth development, they understand that assets in one area reinforce growth in another. Abundant opportunities for learning and exploration in school, after school, and in the community help students mature in all areas.

3. *They offer young people, their families, and community residents opportunities to build social capital.* Social capital connects students to

people and information that can help them solve problems and meet their goals. Community schools enable all students to forge networks and social skills through mentoring relationships with caring adults, school-to-work learning, community service, and other experiences, while providing parents and other adults with similar opportunities to learn and assume leadership roles.[2]

Organization and management

There are three key organization and management functions in a community schools strategy: (1) initiative management and technical assistance, (2) school site planning teams, and (3) community school coordinators.

1. *Initiative management:* Multisite community school initiatives require a core staff. Key tasks for the staff include (1) staffing and supporting community and school leadership, (2) defining the results that the community school seeks to achieve and monitoring progress, (3) building a constituency for community schools, (4) enhancing the capacity of schools and community-based organizations to work together, and (5) ensuring program quality. Cities, counties, school districts, United Ways, and nonprofit institutions all play such a role or help to finance it.[3]

2. *Site-based planning teams:* At the building level, planning and oversight teams that include families and residents, school staff, and community partners provide leadership for individual community schools. The purpose of such teams is to review data, assess existing programs, identify gaps in services, mobilize community resources, monitor progress toward results, and serve as a resource for parent and community engagement in the school.

3. *Community school coordinator:* A community school coordinator mobilizes and integrates school and community resources, improves the impact of these resources on student learning, and frees up the time of principals and teachers. This position enables the school and community partners to develop strong and sustained

relationships. Appointing the coordinator to the school leadership team demonstrates the role's importance and increases its effectiveness.

The federal role in community schools

No federal program is now specifically targeted to support community schools, though many are being used. Two examples are the 21st Century Community Learning Centers Program and the Safe Schools/Healthy Students program. A slew of other programs fund activities at community schools, but there is not a coherent federal framework that connects the array of programs serving children, youth, and families together in a broad agenda that supports student success.

The proposed Full Services Community Schools legislation,[4] introduced by House Democratic Whip Steny Hoyer (Maryland) and Nebraska Senator Ben Nelson, would remedy this situation. The bill authorizes the U.S. Department of Education to fund local grantees to create full-service community schools. Consistent with the principle of partnership underlying community schools, local grantees would have to include a local educational agency and one or more community-based organizations, nonprofit organizations, or other public-private entities. Funds would be awarded to grantees coordinating multiple services at a school site to reduce fragmentation and increase the accessibility of services. Priority is given to grantees that serve at least one school in which at least 40 percent of the children are from low-income families, demonstrate a record of effectiveness, and serve more than one full-service community school.

The state provision also reflects the strategies for state action in support of community schools set forth in the *Coalition for Community School's Handbook for State Policy.*[5]

- *Develop districtwide community school strategies.* The bills give priority to schools and communities that move beyond single-school models to a multiple-school, systemwide effort.

- *Focus on results.* The bills expect successful grantees to define their desired results and track progress toward them.
- *Organize planning teams at the school site.* The bills encourage the use of school-community teams to plan and oversee community school activities.
- *Respect existing school-community governance arrangements.* The bill does not require that any new governance structure be established.
- *Allow communities to pick who will lead the effort.* The bill lets communities select the organization—school, public agency, or nonprofit organization—that has the expertise and demonstrated capacity to lead and manage the community school initiative.
- *Improve coordination of funding streams.* The bill requires coordination at the local level, offers support to states to enhance coordination, and creates a federal interagency group for the same purpose at the federal level.
- *Build community capacity.* Funds could be used to build the infrastructure necessary to sustain community schools: systems to track and report results, technical assistance and professional development, program coordination, and planning and evaluation.

Conclusion

The community school movement has made extraordinary strides in the past fifteen years. More and more policymakers, practitioners, parents, and community residents are doing what this chapter has suggested, in order to create and sustain community schools: focusing on results, developing leadership, finding financing, and building a strong organizational and management capacity. This has all happened in an education policy environment that has become all too narrowly focused on academics.

The Coalition for Community Schools, organized in 1998, provides the policy, research, and advocacy support for the community school movement. More than 170 organizations from education, youth development, health and human services, community development, local government, and philanthropy[6] are now partners in the Coalition.

Ultimately, all of this work at the school, community, state, and national levels must be about advocacy and constituency building. Community school advocates build constituency with parents, students, and residents throughout the community, educate policymakers at the local, state, and federal levels, and show citizens why community schools are a better use of public and private resources. This kind of advocacy will be essential to moving Full Services Community Schools legislation at the federal level, changing policy at the state level, and creating local political will. Ultimately, strengthening and growing the community schools movement is about building constituency and building community.

Notes

1. For more information, see Melaville, A., Shah, A. P., & Blank, M. J. (n.d.). *Making the difference: Research and practice in community schools.* Washington, DC: Coalition for Community Schools. Available at http://www.communityschools.org/mtdhomepage.html.

2. For more information, see Melaville, Shah, & Blank (n.d.).

3. For more information on the work of such intermediaries, see Local Intermediary Organizations: Connecting the Dots for Children, Youth and Families (www.communityschools.org/Toolkit/Intermediaries.pdf).

4. The Full Services Community Schools Act was introduced in the 108th Congress. It will be reintroduced in the 109th Congress. For the new version, see the Web site of the Democrat Whip Steny Hoyer (www.hoyer.house.gov/) or Senator Ben Nelson (bennelson.senate.gov/) or www.communityschools.org.

5. State Policy Handbook. (2002). *A handbook for state policy leaders.* Available at http://www.communityschools.org/Resources/handbook.pdf.

6. For a list of Coalition partners, see www.communityschools.org and click on "Who We Are."

MARTY BLANK *is director of the Coalition for Community Schools at the Institute for Educational Leadership.*

Afterword

Joy Dryfoos

IN THIS VOLUME, a variety of practitioners have shared their experiences in developing full-service community schools. We can learn a lot from these people about how to approach the challenges in building partnerships between schools and community agencies at the school, community, state, and national levels.

I had a professor a long time ago at Antioch College who was fond of reminding us, "If you don't know where you're going, any road will take you there." The first lesson that can be drawn from these accounts is the importance of a common vision, a detailed road map that specifies where the stakeholders want to go. This mapping and planning has to involve a broad array of players. Obviously, the school system, as well as community-based agencies, the political powers (mayor, council members), the teachers' union, university partners, parents—and even students—must all have a role in conducting needs assessments and designing community schools.

Another lesson is that leadership for such an initiative can come from almost anywhere. What makes community schools an emerging "field" is the consensus among its advocates that life can and must be better for young people and that youth development can be fostered more effectively in new kinds of responsive social institutions. Schools have become the place to implement youth development concepts and to apply the critical dosages of hands-on nurturing and caring, as well as social-emotional learning.

These communitywide efforts start in many different places: social agencies, universities, city or county governments, state governments, superintendents' offices, or right at a school. In Evansville, one principal in one school "full-serviced" her school, thus

NEW DIRECTIONS FOR YOUTH DEVELOPMENT, NO. 107, FALL 2005 © WILEY PERIODICALS, INC.

providing a model for the whole community to emulate. Principals are probably the most critical element in developing community schools. They are the guardians of the access points—access to the children, use and maintenance of the facility, and involvement of the teachers. They promote integration of what's already there in the classroom with what gets brought in by the outside agencies. They set the tone for the whole school. Hopefully, as the word spreads about community schools, more principals will take the initiative and invite partners to provide services.

Of course, the bottom line in all these narratives is "relationships." Everyone has to talk to everyone else frequently, and the talk often has to be backed up with a memorandum of agreement or a contract. Talk takes time and patience. Meetings are endemic. Just imagine what it takes to move a primary-care health clinic into a school building. The school has to want the facility, make space for it, and have the ability to maintain it. The health care provider must be identified and procedures agreed upon. When the plan is ready and the Board of Health has given clearance, building renovation takes place, and equipment is purchased. When the clinic opens and the outside staff moves in, arrangements have to be made to delineate and coordinate the functions of the clinic staff in relationship to existing school support personnel.

I am fortunate to have had the opportunity to visit many of the programs mentioned in this issue. What I find particularly impressive is the ingenuity of the practitioners in addressing the needs of the students and their families. For example, the University of Pennsylvania's Health Promotion and Disease Prevention Program brings faculty and students into the school to teach health classes; the program trains high school students to become health advocates in the community. California's Healthy Start supports schools that provide food and clothing and others that work on transportation issues. Parents are trained to do outreach in the neighborhood. The Children's Aid Society (CAS) brings the settlement house into the school, with particular sensitivity to the culture of the local community.

Sustainability is an ongoing challenge. Funding is necessary for moving a clinic into a school or operating a parent center or offering before- and after-school programs. Funding is essential for hiring a full-time coordinator for each participating community school and for staffing a communitywide coordinating organization. Each of the initiatives has put together a different package of funding, drawing from whatever resources are available in that specific community. Almost all use 21st Century Community Learning Center dollars for after-school programs and parent education, and some tap other federal sources such as Safe and Drug Free Schools. In Chicago, school funds are designated for community schools, and they also use Supplemental Education Services funds from No Child Left Behind. In Portland, the County Department of School and Community Partnerships, as well as the City of Portland, support the SUN Initiative. The Beacons receive core support through the New York City Department of Youth and Community Development.

Foundations play a major role in the development of community schools. Many of these community coalitions came into existence under the auspices of foundation grants. The Public Education Network school-community partnership project resulted from a substantial grant from the Annenberg Foundation. By engaging broad constituencies across communities, local education funds have been able to build strong relationships between and among community institutions.

Chicago has moved ahead rapidly because of substantial foundation support, first for demonstration sites and later for wider replication. The Boston Full-Service Schools Roundtable was able to hire an executive director and consultants when three local foundations quickly responded to proposals.

Most of these initiatives have some form of evaluation, although many of the studies are in early stages. Collectively, they show good results in child well-being, family functioning, access to health services, and reduction in high-risk behaviors. Only a few sites can demonstrate significant improvements in achievement attributable to being a community school. However, as the programs strengthen and the components become more thoroughly integrated, it is expected that achievement will improve in more places.

I believe that the full-service community school concept will become very important in school reform and youth development. Initiatives like these are proliferating, and local coalitions are taking on the whole school system rather than one school at a time. A few states are beginning to wake up and get interested, with the charge to coordinate fragmented state-level agencies and pool education, after-school, health, mental health, social service, prevention, and juvenile justice resources. At the national level, the Full Services Community Schools Act has recently been introduced by Senators Steny Hoyer and Ben Nelson, and it is possible that this new field will gain visibility. If the legislation is passed, grants will become available to local school-community partnerships and to state governments ($200 million a year). Advocates for the 21st Century Community Learning Centers program are currently working to convince Congress to appropriate funds to the level authorized under the No Child Left Behind legislation in 2002, which would increase funding for the program from the current $1 billion to $2.5 billion by FY 2007. And these same advocates will continue to work on expansion of funding when NCLB is reauthorized (now slated for 2007). Internationally, community schools are very popular, with many countries, including England, Scotland, and The Netherlands, receiving wide support from their governments.

The people who contributed to this volume are leading the way, taking their initiatives "to scale." It would be foolish to deny that this is hard work. I have to admit that I am glad to write about it, but I could never have the patience and the fortitude to do it. To sum up the effort: it takes recruitment of the necessary stakeholders, months of planning and negotiation, years of grant writing, endless hours of implementation (meetings!), careful selection of personnel, ingenuity in finding the right components for each school, cultural sensitivity, participation in advocacy, and long-term commitment. All of this labor produces exciting and innovative schools that are open most of the time, full of stimulated students and involved parents who can access needed support. Neighborhoods improve. Teachers are happier because they have help overcoming barriers to learning. I believe community school people would advise you that this is an effort well worth making.

JOY DRYFOOS *is an independent writer from Brookline, Massachusetts.*

Index

Notes for Contributors

New Directions for Youth Development: Theory, Practice, and Research is a quarterly publication focusing on contemporary issues challenging the field of youth development. A defining focus of the journal is the relationship among theory, research, and practice. In particular, *NDYD* is dedicated to recognizing resilience as well as risk, and healthy development of our youth as well as the difficulties of adolescence. The journal is intended as a forum for provocative discussion that reaches across the worlds of academia, service, philanthropy, and policy.

In the tradition of the New Directions series, each volume of the journal addresses a single, timely topic, although special issues covering a variety of topics are occasionally commissioned. We welcome submissions of both volume topics and individual articles. All articles should specifically address the implications of theory for practice and research directions, and how these arenas can better inform one another. Articles may focus on any aspect of youth development; all theoretical and methodological orientations are welcome.

If you would like to be an *issue editor*, please submit an outline of no more than four pages that includes a brief description of your proposed topic and its significance along with a brief synopsis of individual articles (including tentative authors and a working title for each chapter).

If you would like to be an *author*, please submit first a draft of an abstract of no more than 1,500 words, including a two-sentence synopsis of the article; send this to the managing editor.

For all prospective issue editors or authors:

- Please make sure to keep accessibility in mind, by illustrating theoretical ideas with specific examples and explaining technical terms in nontechnical language. A busy practitioner who may not have an extensive research background should be well served by our work.

- Please keep in mind that references should be limited to twenty-five to thirty. Authors should make use of case examples to illustrate their ideas, rather than citing exhaustive research references. You may want to recommend two or three key articles, books, or Websites that are influential in the field, to be featured on a resource page. This can be used by readers who want to delve more deeply into a particular topic.
- All reference information should be listed as endnotes, rather than including author names in the body of the article or footnotes at the bottom of the page. The endnotes are in APA style.

Please visit http://www.ndyd.org for more information.

Gil G. Noam
Editor-in-Chief

Back Issue/Subscription Order Form

Copy or detach and send to:

Jossey-Bass, A Wiley Company, 989 Market Street, San Francisco, CA 94103-1741

Call or fax toll-free: Phone 888-378-2537 6:30AM – 3PM PST; Fax 888-481-2665

Back Issues: Please send me the following issues at $29 each
(Important: please include series initials and issue number, such as YD100.)

_____

_____

_____

$ _____   Total for single issues

$ _____   SHIPPING CHARGES: SURFACE   Domestic   Canadian

	Domestic	Canadian
First Item	$5.00	$6.00
Each Add'l Item	$3.00	$1.50

For next-day and second-day delivery rates, call the number listed above.

Subscriptions: Please __start __renew my subscription to *New Directions for Youth Development* for the year 2_____ at the following rate:

U.S.	__Individual $80	__Institutional $180
Canada	__Individual $80	__Institutional $220
All Others	__Individual $104	__Institutional $254

**For more information about online subscriptions visit
www.interscience.wiley.com**

$ _____   Total single issues and subscriptions (Add appropriate sales tax for your state for single issue orders. No sales tax for U.S. subscriptions. Canadian residents, add GST for subscriptions and single issues.)

__Payment enclosed (U.S. check or money order only)
__VISA __MC __AmEx #_____ Exp. Date _____

Signature _____ Day Phone _____
__ Bill Me (U.S. institutional orders only. Purchase order required.)

Purchase order # _____
           Federal Tax ID13559302   **GST 89102 8052**

Name _____

Address _____

_____

Phone _____ E-mail _____

For more information about Jossey-Bass, visit our Web site at **www.josseybass.com**

Other Titles Available

NEW DIRECTIONS FOR YOUTH DEVELOPMENT: THEORY, PRACTICE, AND RESEARCH
Gil G. Noam, Editor-in-Chief

YD106 **Putting Youth at the Center of Community Building**
Joel Nitzberg, Editor
This issue offers an explanation of community-building principles
and how they can be applied working with youth. The chapter
authors provide examples of how community building can be connected to youth development and how youth can be change agents.
A challenge underlying this approach is to help communities engage
youth in change efforts that are meaningful to them. This may mean
expanding youth expression in ways that influence community
behavior. It also means looking for ways for youth to develop and
use leadership skills to influence change. Contributors show how the
community-building field emphasizes the importance of networking
and building relationships, enabling all members of a community to
potentially be change agents.
ISBN: 0-7879-8157-5

YD105 **Participation in Youth Programs: Enrollment, Attendance,
and Engagement**
Heather B. Weiss, Priscilla M. D. Little, Suzanne M. Bouffard, Editors
This timely volume proposes that to understand and intervene to
improve participation in out-of-school time (OST) programs, issues
of access, enrollment, and engagement must be considered, and in the
context of program quality. Contributing authors pose a three-part
equation where participation = enrollment + attendance + engagement,
and examine these three critical components of overall participation
in out-of-school time programs. Chapters provide research-based
strategies on how to increase participation, and how to define, measure, and study it, drawing from the latest developmental research and
evaluation literature.
ISBN: 0-7879-8053-6

YD104 **Professional Development for Youth Workers**
Pam Garza, Lynne M. Borden, Kirk A. Astroth
Professional development of caring, capable adults who interact with
and on behalf of youth is a key issue for youth organizations and agencies committed to creating environments that nurture young people's

growth and transition into adulthood. This issue offers a glimpse of some of the innovated, sustained, and coordinated efforts to advance the preparation and support of youth workers based on the principles of positive youth development. Contributors provide examples demonstrating how to support youth work interaction as well as training networks that take common approaches to professional development and outline some of the significant challenges faced in youth worker professional development and their solutions. From defining competencies for entry-level youth workers to case studies that explore the role of colleges and universities in professionalizing the field, this issue serves as a record of the evolution of the youth development field and a call for its continued progress in building a comprehensive system that can meet the needs of both youth workers and the young people they come into contact with each day.
ISBN 0-7879-7861-2

YD103   **The Transforming Power of Adult-Youth Relationships**
Gil G. Noam, Nina Fiore
Introducing various perspectives that look at the changes in theories, attitudes, approaches, and practices in adult-youth relationships, this issue stresses a model of growth based on partnership and connection over older theories of autonomy and hierarchy between adults and youth. These ways of viewing young people's contributions as extremely important to societal development have to be increasingly embedded in a perspective that young people grow and thrive in relationships and that social institutions, especially families, schools, and youth-serving organizations, have to change dramatically. Contributors also demonstrate how much common ground exists between older and emerging models of youth development and how much work remains to be done.
ISBN 0-7879-7788-8

YD102   **Negotiation: Interpersonal Approaches to Intergroup Conflict**
Daniel L. Shapiro, Brooke E. Clayton
This issue considers the emotional complexities of intergroup conflict. The chapter authors examine the relational challenges that youth encounter in dealing with conflict and, combining innovative theory with ambitious practical application, identify conflict management strategies. These interventions have affected millions of youth across the continents.
ISBN 0-7879-7649-0

YD101   **After-School Worlds: Creating a New Social Space for Development and Learning**
Gil G. Noam
Showcases a variety of large-scale policy initiatives, effective institutional collaborations, and innovative programming options that produce high-quality environments in which young people are

YD94   **Youth Development and After-School Time: A Tale of Many Cities**
Gil G. Noam, Beth Miller
This issue looks at exciting citywide and cross-city initiatives in after-school time. It presents case studies of youth-related work that combines large-scale policy, developmental thinking, and innovative programming, as well as research and evaluation. Chapters discuss efforts of community-based organizations, museums, universities, schools, and clinics who are joining forces, sharing funding and other resources, and jointly creating a system of after-school care and education.
ISBN 0-7879-6337-2

YD93   **A Critical View of Youth Mentoring**
Jean E. Rhodes
Mentoring has become an almost essential aspect of youth develop-ment and is expanding beyond the traditional one-to-one, volunteer, community-based mentoring. This volume provides evidence of the benefits of enduring high-quality mentoring programs, as well as apprenticeships, advisories, and other relationship-based programs that show considerable promise. Authors examine mentoring in the workplace, teacher-student interaction, and the mentoring poten-tial of student advising programs. They also take a critical look at the importance of youth-adult relationships and how a deeper understanding of these relationships can benefit youth mentoring. This issue raises important questions about relationship-based interventions and generates new perspectives on the role of adults in the lives of youth.
ISBN 0-7879-6294-5

YD92   **Zero Tolerance: Can Suspension and Expulsion Keep Schools Safe?**
Russell J. Skiba, Gil G. Noam
Addressing the problem of school violence and disruption requires thoughtful understanding of the complexity of the personal and systemic factors that increase the probability of violence, and designing interventions based on that understanding. This inaugural issue explores the effectiveness of zero tolerance as a tool for pro-moting school safety and improving student behavior and offers alternative strategies that work.
ISBN 0-7879-1441-X

NEW DIRECTIONS FOR YOUTH DEVELOPMENT
IS NOW AVAILABLE ONLINE AT WILEY INTERSCIENCE

What is Wiley InterScience?

Wiley InterScience is the dynamic online content service from John Wiley & Sons delivering the full text of over 300 leading scientific, technical, medical, and professional journals, plus major reference works, the acclaimed *Current Protocols* laboratory manuals, and even the full text of select Wiley print books online.

What are some special features of Wiley InterScience?

Wiley InterScience Alerts is a service that delivers table of contents via e-mail for any journal available on Wiley InterScience as soon as a new issue is published online.
Early View is Wiley's exclusive service presenting individual articles online as soon as they are ready, even before the release of the compiled print issue. These articles are complete, peer-reviewed, and citable.
CrossRef is the innovative multi-publisher reference linking system enabling readers to move seamlessly from a reference in a journal article to the cited publication, typically located on a different server and published by a different publisher.

How can I access Wiley InterScience?

Visit http://www.interscience.wiley.com

Guest Users can browse Wiley InterScience for unrestricted access to journal Tables of Contents and Article Abstracts, or use the powerful search engine.
Registered Users are provided with a *Personal Home Page* to store and manage customized alerts, searches, and links to favorite journals and articles. Additionally, Registered Users can view free Online Sample Issues and preview selected material from major reference works.
Licensed Customers are entitled to access full-text journal articles in PDF, with select journals also offering full-text HTML.

How do I become an Authorized User?

Authorized Users are individuals authorized by a paying Customer to have access to the journals in Wiley InterScience. For example, a university that subscribes to Wiley journals is considered to be the Customer. Faculty, staff and students authorized by the university to have access to those journals in Wiley InterScience are Authorized Users. Users should contact their Library for information on which Wiley journals they have access to in Wiley InterScience.

ASK YOUR INSTITUTION ABOUT WILEY INTERSCIENCE TODAY!

incident has occurred as well as preparing children for future threats in ways that enhance feelings of safety rather than raise anxiety.
ISBN 0-7879-7075-1

YD97 **When, Where, What, and How Youth Learn**
Karen J. Pittman, Nicole Yohalem, Joel Tolman
Acknowledging that young people learn throughout their waking hours, in a range of settings, and through a variety of means, this volume presents practical advancements, theory development and new research in policies and infrastructures that support expanded definitions of learning. Representing the perspectives of a broad range of scholars and practitioners, chapters explore ways to connect learning experiences that happen inside and outside school buildings and during and after the school day. The contributors offer a compelling argument that communitywide commitments to learning are necessary if our nation's young people are to become problem free, fully prepared, and fully engaged.
ISBN 0-7879-6848-X

YD96 **Youth Participation: Improving Institutions and Communities**
Benjamin Kirshner, Jennifer L. O'Donoghue, Milbrey McLaughlin
Explores the growing effort in youth organizations, community development, and schools and other public institutions to foster meaningful activities that empower adolescents to participate in decision making that affects their lives and to take action on issues they care about. Pushing against long-held, culturally specific ideas about adolescence as well as institutional barriers to youth involvement, the efforts of these organizations engaged in youth participation programs deserve careful analysis and support. This volume offers an assessment of the field, as well as specific chapters that chronicle efforts to achieve youth participation across a variety of settings and dimensions.
ISBN 0-7879-6339-9

YD95 **Pathways to Positive Development Among Diverse Youth**
Richard M. Lerner, Carl S. Taylor, Alexander von Eye
Positive youth development represents an emerging emphasis in developmental thinking that is focused on the incredible potential of adolescents to maintain healthy trajectories and develop resilience, even in the face of myriad negative influences. This volume discusses the theory, research, policy, and programs that take this strength-based, positive development approach to diverse youth. Examines theoretical ideas about the nature of positive youth development, and about the related concepts of thriving and well-being, as well as current and needed policy strategies, "best practice" in youth-serving programs, and promising community-based efforts to marshal the developmental assets of individuals and communities to enhance thriving among youth.
ISBN 0-7879-6338-0

realizing their potential. Contributors underscore the conditions—
from fostering interagency partnerships, to structuring organized
out-of-school-time activities, to encouraging staff-student relationships—that lay the groundwork for positive youth development after
school. At the same time, their examples illuminate the challenges
for policymakers, researchers, and educators to redefine the field of
afterschool as a whole, including the search for a shared lexicon, the
push to preserve the character of afterschool as an intermediary
space, and the need to create and further programs that are grounded
in reliable research and that demonstrate success.
ISBN 0-7879-7304-1

YD100 **Understanding the Social Worlds of Immigrant Youth**
Carola Suárez-Orozco, Irina L. G. Todorova
This issue seeks to deepen understanding of the major social influences that shape immigrant youths' paths in their transition to the
United States. The authors delve into a number of social worlds that
can contribute to the positive development of immigrant youth.
They also provide insight into sources of information about identity
pathway options available to those youth. The chapters offer new
data regarding the developmental opportunities that family roles and
responsibilities, school contexts, community organizations, religious
involvement and beliefs, gendered expectations, and media influences
present.
ISBN 0-7879-7267-3

YD99 **Deconstructing the School-to-Prison Pipeline**
Johanna Wald, Daniel J. Losen
This issue describes how school policies can have the effect, if not
the intent, of setting youths on the "prison track." It also identifies
programs and policies that can help schools maintain safety and
order while simultaneously reaching out to those students most in
need of structure, education, and guidance. Offering a balanced perspective, this issue begins to point the way toward less punitive, more
effective, hopeful directions.
ISBN 0-7879-7227-4

YD98 **Youth Facing Threat and Terror: Supporting Preparedness
and Resilience**
Robert D. Macy, Susanna Barry, Gil G. Noam
Intended to help clinicians, youth and community workers, teachers,
and parents to support resolution and recovery, this volume examines
the effects of threat, stress, and traumatic events, including acts of terror, on children and youth. It addresses not only the individual reper-
cussions of threat but also a collective approach to threat. It also
illustrates important ways to prevent traumatic situations from having lifelong, negative impacts. These methods involve providing
immediate intervention and fostering safety as soon as a threatening